Steroids, Sports, and Body Image

The Risks of Performance-Enhancing Drugs

Judy Monroe

Enslow Publishers, Inc.

40 Industrial Road	PO Box 38
Box 398	Aldershot
Berkeley Heights, NJ 07922	Hants GU12 6BP
USA	UK

http://www.enslow.com

Library of Congress Cataloging-in-Publication Data

Monroe, Judy.
    Steroids, sports, and body image : the risks of performance-enhancing drugs / Judy Monroe.
        v. cm.—(Issues in focus)
    Includes bibliographical references and index.
    Contents: Making world headlines—What are anabolic steroids?—Who's using?—Health consequences—Steroids and body image—Steroids and sports—Laws—Continuing controversy.
    ISBN 0-7660-2160-2
    1. Anabolic steroids—Health aspects. 2. Doping in sports.
3. Body image. 4. Steroids. [1. Steroids. 2. Drug abuse.
3. Athletes—Drug use. 4. Body image.] I. Title. II. Issues in focus
(Berkeley Heights, N.J.)
    RC1230.M673   2004
    362.29'088'796—dc22
                                                    2003026605

Printed in the United States of America

10 9 8 7 6 5 4 3 2 1

To Our Readers: We have done our best to make sure all Internet addresses in this book were active and appropriate when we went to press. However, the author and the publisher have no control over and assume no liability for the material available on those Internet sites or on other Web sites they may link to. Any comments or suggestions can be sent by e-mail to comments@enslow.com or to the address on the back cover.

Illustration Credits: AP/Wide World, pp. 7, 106; Jeff Bartle, p. 111; Catherine Behrendt, p. 102; Corel Corp., pp. 10, 37, 62, 75, 80, 86, 90; Courtesy of Kidney Foundation of Canada, p. 48; Library of Congress, p. 70; National Archives, p. 17; National Institute of Drug Abuse, National Institutes of Health, p. 42; Rubberball Productions, p. 56; Owen Sanders, pp. 24, 32, 54; Stockbyte, p. 66.

Cover Illustration: Thinkstock

Contents

Making World Headlines

In September 1988, Ben Johnson, a Canadian sprinter, stunned the world—twice. At the 1988 Summer Olympic Games in Seoul, South Korea, he and a handful of other athletes competed in the 100-meter dash. He considered this event his specialty. Only his arch rival, American sprinter Carl Lewis, promised to be a tough competitor.

After the starting pistol sounded, Johnson ran his best race ever. He crossed the finish line at an amazing 9.79 seconds. Fellow Canadians and others fans cheered the world's fastest man. Johnson received the Olympic gold medal. Carl

Lewis captured the silver medal, or second place, by clocking in at 9.92 seconds. That was just 13/100 of a second behind Johnson.

Soon after the race, Johnson tested positive for an anabolic steroid called stanozolol. Anabolic steroids are powerful, man-made drugs that can help people develop bigger muscles. When not properly prescribed by a doctor, they are illegal for people to take.

To the shame of his country, Johnson was stripped of his gold medal. Lewis was declared the winner. The Canadian sprinter received further punishment: He was not allowed to run in international races for two years.

Due, in part, to Ben Johnson, 1988 was called the "Year of Steroids." Also, many other athletes were caught taking anabolic steroids at the 1988 Olympics and other sporting events that year. The year 1988 marked the first time that anabolic steroids, or steroids as they are commonly called, became a household word.

Not Allowed

For a superstar like Ben Johnson to be stripped of his gold medal because of steroid abuse made big news in 1988. The International Olympic Committee (IOC) had officially banned steroids in 1975. Athletes continued to use them, though. As a result, more and more associations banned steroids.

The allure of steroids still continues to beckon athletes today. Some athletes, both amateur and professional, want to win so much that they are willing

Ben Johnson gives the "number one" sign after setting a world record for the men's hundred-meter dash in the 1988 Olympics. A short time later, he tested positive for steroids and lost his gold medal.

to take drugs to gain an advantage. So they turn to steroids.

Steroids are powerful drugs. They are a form of testosterone, a natural hormone found in males and, in smaller amounts, in females. These drugs have been proven to increase muscle size quickly and can promote weight gain.

Scientists still debate if steroids can enhance performance. Health professionals know that using steroids illegally can lead to a variety of side effects (unintended effects) and can sometimes increase aggressive behavior. Street names or slang terms for anabolic steroids include roids, hype, pump, arnolds, gym candy, pumpers, stackers, weight trainers, gear, the sauce, or juice.

Today, all anabolic steroids are banned from athletic competition. They are not supposed to be used to improve performance in sporting events. Yet some athletes use steroids, even though they know that they could be eliminated from competition or lose a medal. Since 1988, the glory of each Olympic game has been marred by some athletes testing positive for steroids. These athletes have not been allowed to compete.

Ben Johnson, the former world-famous runner, returned to competition in 1991. He tried to place in the 100-meter final at the 1992 Olympic Games, held in Barcelona, Spain. This time he did not take drugs. He said, "I wanted to prove the impossible, that I could win by doing the opposite of everyone else— staying clean."[1] Johnson, though, failed to qualify.

Johnson tried competitive running once more, in

January 1993. After a Montreal meet, Johnson was found to have excessive levels of testosterone. This time, he was banned for life from competitive sports.

Ben Johnson's punishment for steroid use did not stop some athletes from using them. These drugs may tempt teen athletes at a time when they are looking for a performance edge. Some may want to play well, hoping to earn a sports scholarship to college. Aside from a scholarship, some want individual glory and attention. Others want to concentrate on the glory of winning for their high school team or sport.

"Where I suspect I am seeing signs of steroid use is during screening physicals for junior college teams," said Aynsley Smith, Ph.D. Smith is at the Sports Medicine Center at the Mayo Clinic in Rochester, Minnesota. Before players are signed up to be on a team, they go through a physical exam. During this screening, players are examined for physical fitness as well as illegal drug use. "Many of these players are hoping they'll still catch on at a 4-year school. They look ripped [muscular], and I see lots of stretch marks, but not like they've been working hard in the gym."[2] Stretch marks mean that the muscle has grown very quickly. As a result, the skin is stretched and develops marks.

Looking for Perfection

Beyond athletes, another group of people use steroids, too, and in growing numbers. Teens and adults, both male and female, want to look more

Most athletes depend on training and practice for improvement, but some rely on steroids as well.

attractive. In their quest for a particular body type, they turn to steroids to help them achieve their goal. Steroids may help some develop bigger muscles and a leaner body. However, the price of using these drugs illegally may be high.

Various side effects can result, ranging from acne to life-threatening diseases. In addition, it is illegal to sell or buy prescription steroids for nonmedical use. Possession of steroids for nonmedical use is also illegal. Anabolic steroids are legal if prescribed by a physician. For those who want to get them illegally, they can click a computer mouse. Steroids are a big business in the United States. They can be ordered on the Internet and through mail order from Europe, Canada, Thailand, and Mexico, where these drugs are legal. Sometimes dealers at competitions, health clubs, and gyms sell to buyers.

A 2001 survey by the National Collegiate Athletic Association (NCAA) showed this growing trend. This study looked at the substance-use habits of college student-athletes. Researchers asked 21,225 students at 713 institutions why they used anabolic steroids. Most steroid users reported that they took the drugs to improve their athletic performance. In addition, the researchers found that "many users are now stating they use anabolic steroids to improve appearance."[3]

2

What Are Anabolic Steroids?

A limited number of anabolic steroids have been approved for medical and veterinary use. The main legitimate use of these drugs in humans is to replace inadequate levels of testosterone that result from a reduction or absence of functioning testes, the male sex organs. A huge black (illegal) market exists for anabolic steroids.

Steroids Defined

Steroids are hormones. These hormones are sometimes called the chemical messengers of the body. All steroids have a similar basic chemical structure that is much like

12

cholesterol. (The human body makes cholesterol, a waxy substance that has a role in heart disease.) The adrenal glands, located on top of the kidneys, and the ovaries and testes, the reproductive organs, secrete hormones.

The body produces a variety of hormones that help control metabolism, inflammation (swelling), and function of the immune system. Hormones also balance salt and water, contribute to the development of sexual characteristics, and help people deal with the stress of illness and injury.

Certain hormones work on specific organs. Four examples of natural hormones are growth hormone, insulin, estrogen, and testosterone. Growth hormone makes the bones grow longer. Insulin controls the absorption of glucose, an energy source of the body, by cells. Estrogen, the female sex hormone, produces such effects as soft skin, wider hips, and breasts. Estrogen also causes pubic and underarm hair to grow.

Only a tiny amount of testosterone, the male sex hormone, is needed to produce sexual function. Testosterone is in both males and females. The average adult male produces 2.5 to 11 milligrams of testosterone each day. Such a small amount can only be seen with the aid of a microscope. Testosterone's anabolic, or building, effects help the body retain dietary protein. This aids in the growth of muscles, bone, and skin. Testosterone's androgenic, or masculinizing, properties promote growth of body hair, deepening of the voice, and sex drive. It can also affect aggressiveness.

Females produce much less of this hormone than males, just a trace amount. This is about one seventh of the male's amount. Production of testosterone in females occurs in the ovaries and the adrenal glands. In males, the testes produce nearly all of the testosterone. In both sexes, testosterone helps maintain muscle and bone and contributes to sexual function.

Females who take anabolic steroids have less body fat. That is due to testosterone, which makes males have less body fat than women. So, a woman who takes steroids will grow leaner and develop bigger muscles. Her body will begin to look more like a man's body.

Defining Anabolic Steroids

Anabolic steroids are also called anabolic-androgenic steroids. They are man-made or synthetic versions of testosterone and are chemically related. Someone who takes anabolic steroids illegally is likely to gain weight, build muscles, and get stronger.

Anabolic steroids have two basic effects:

- an androgenic effect—causes the development of male features such as facial and body hair growth, deepening of the voice, and development of the testes and penis.

- an anabolic effect—builds skeletal muscle tissue. Muscles use steroids to grow and build muscles.

You may have heard of medicines called steroids that reduce inflammation and swelling. These are called corticosteroids. They are not the same as anabolic steroids. Corticosteroids mimic the effects of two hormones, cortisone and hydrocortisone. Both hormones are made by the outer layer of the adrenal glands.

Corticosteroids are used to treat common medical conditions such as asthma and arthritis, or inflammation of the joints. Although strong medications, corticosteroids are not abused by athletes and others because they do not build muscle.

History of Anabolic Steroids

In the late 1800s, scientists began to search for the substance that gives men their male characteristics. They tested various chemicals found in the testes. During this time, a French doctor named Charles-Édouard Brown-Séquard injected himself with an extract made from the testicles of guinea pigs and dogs. He claimed that this mixture gave him strength and energy. However, no active hormones actually existed in his preparation, so his claim was untrue.

Scientists continued their quest. In the early 1930s, German scientists identified a substance similar to testosterone. They extracted this substance by collecting thousands of liters of urine from male policemen. They were searching for a substance made by the testes, but never found it.

Finally in 1935, Dutch scientists in Amsterdam made history. That year, they identified a substance from bull testes that they called testosterone. Other scientists quickly learned how to make this substance in their laboratories. Now artificial testosterone was available in large amounts. At first, doctors used testosterone mostly for two reasons:

- To treat malnutrition. Some malnourished people developed hypogonadism, a condition where the testes do not produce enough testosterone for normal growth, development, and sexual functioning.

- To promote healing after surgery.

Scientists soon discovered that this powerful drug could stimulate the growth of skeletal muscle in laboratory animals. By 1939, researchers had found that testosterone could enhance physical performance. Other scientists, though, warned of possible dangers. That same year, a scientist said that the use of steroids, "should definitely be avoided since it may involve dangers the extent of which cannot be entirely gauged."[1]

As word of testosterone's powers spread, its use increased. German soldiers during World War II (1939–1945) supposedly took this drug to increase aggressiveness. No written record of these tests exists, however. After World War II ended in 1945, doctors gave this drug to the many starving people who had been held by the Nazis in concentration camps. These drugs helped prisoners, who were severely malnourished and thin, build up their body weight and regain their health quickly.

In 1954, reports of steroids used by athletes in a sport hit the news. World weight-lifting champions in Vienna, Austria, were reported to be using this drug.

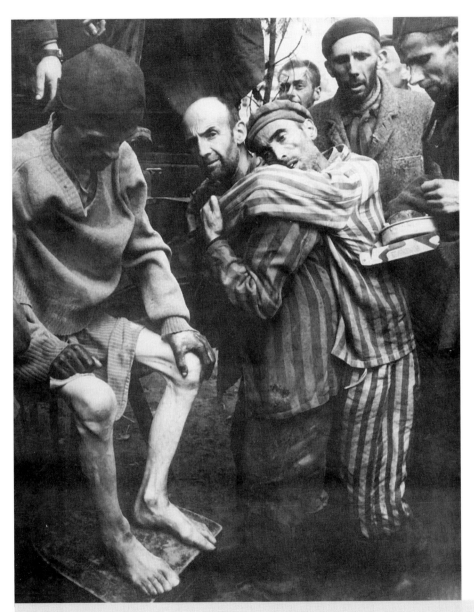

Nazi concentration camp survivors like these men were often given steroids to help them build muscle and strength.

About the same time, Russian doctors began giving testosterone to their athletes because it seemed to help build muscle. In response, the United States coach, Dr. John Ziegler, encouraged United States weight lifters to take testosterone. As more bodybuilders and weight lifters heard about testosterone, some started to take the drug. Athletes in other sports began using testosterone, too.

Because of the androgenic effects of testosterone, particularly in women and children, scientists set out to develop synthetic steroids that were less androgenic. They succeeded in 1953 by creating a form of testosterone called 19-nortestosterone, also known as nandrolone. This substance had three to five times the muscle-building effects of testosterone.[2]

Nandrolone became the first drug to be called an anabolic steroid. Since then, all synthetic anabolic steroids have been derived, or originated, from testosterone or nandrolone.

Manufacture of Anabolic Steroids

One limitation of using natural testosterone is that it must be obtained from the testicles of animals. Doctors cannot get enough natural hormone to treat certain diseases in people. Another limitation is that natural testosterone does not work very long when given as a pill or by injection. Natural testosterone is rapidly broken down by the body. So, drug companies make artificial anabolic steroids. Currently, scientists have developed more than a hundred different anabolic steroids.

All steroids require a prescription to be sold and used legally in the United States. At one time, doctors in the United States prescribed anabolic steroids for their patients more liberally. Researchers and the public were not aware of the dangers of these drugs. However, the United States Congress passed a law that made steroids a controlled substance, so this limited their accepted medical uses. Today doctors can only prescribe steroids for the "treatment of disease pursuant to the order of a physician."[3] Enhancing athletic performance clearly does not fit this definition.

Some veterinarians have filled the void left by doctors. Veterinarians routinely use anabolic steroids, especially for horses. They give steroids to horses to treat injuries, but they mainly use steroids to enhance the performance of the horses. This has caused great debate in the horse-racing world. Some states have restricted the use of steroids as performance enhancers for horses.

Sources of Illegal Steroids

Many steroids used in the United States are illegally used. They come from three sources:

- They are smuggled in from other countries. This is the main source of illegal anabolic steroids sold in the United States. Various countries around the world make legal and illegal steroids including Mexico, Canada, Thailand, and Europe. In 1991, Canada revised its laws to make the supply of illegal steroids less available in the United States. After that, the flow of illegal Canadian steroids into the United States lessened somewhat.

- Pharmacies in the United States carry or stock legal steroids. Then these drugs are sometimes illegally stolen from the pharmacies and sold on the black market. Veterinarians have also become sources for people seeking anabolic steroids for their own personal use.

- Some people produce steroids in illegal laboratories. These so-called steroids sometimes contain no anabolic steroids. Others contain an anabolic steroid, but not the same type or amount as stated on the package or label on the container.

Here is a list of the most commonly abused anabolic steroids. All of these are made legally by various drug companies.

Oral Anabolic Steroids

- Anadrol (oxymetholone)

- Oxandrin (oxandrolone)

- Dianabol (methandrostenolone)

- Winstrol (stanozolol)

Injectable Steroids

- Deca-Durabolin (nandrolone decanoate)

- Durabolin (nandrolone phenpropionate)

- Depo-Testosterone (testosterone cypionate)

- Equipoise (boldenone undecylenate)

Many of the testosterone drugs are more anabolic than androgenic. (That is, they produce muscle rather than masculine characteristics). Yet all anabolic steroids can produce androgenic effects if used in high doses. Scientists do not yet know exactly how steroids help build muscle.[4]

Medical Uses for Steroids

A limited number of anabolic steroids have been approved for medical use. Doctors never prescribe anabolic steroids to build muscle in young, healthy people. However, doctors sometimes prescribe these powerful drugs to treat a specific medical problem or disease. Most of these medical uses are uncommon, either because the condition is rare or because other treatments are preferable.

Doctors must use steroids carefully and in small amounts because steroids can produce many side effects. In addition, patients usually take only one type of anabolic steroid at a time, not a combination of types.

The most accepted medical use for anabolic steroids is to treat males unable to produce normal levels of their own testosterone. This condition is called testosterone deficiency, or hypogonadism. Some men who have had testicular cancer may have their testes removed. They are then given oral anabolic steroids to replace the testosterone that their bodies can no longer make. This maintains their male characteristics such as a deep voice.

Doctors also use anabolic steroids to treat a rare

skin condition known as hereditary angioedema and some types of blood diseases such as anemia, a condition where the red blood cell count is too low. When anabolic steroids are combined with female hormones, they can be used to treat some serious symptoms of menopause.

Steroids can also help people who cannot produce muscle or whose muscle has broken down. This occurs in people who have had certain kinds of surgery or cancer, serious burns, or AIDS. The use of anabolic steroids to treat AIDS patients has been growing since the 1990s. In fact, they are becoming the standard treatment for HIV.[5] Steroids help build muscle, improve sexual function, increase the appetite, and decrease depression. These drugs seem to be safe when prescribed and monitored by doctors and medical tests. With exercise, diet, and prescribed anabolic steroids, people with AIDS may be able to build up their muscle tissue, and look and feel better.

Steroids are also used to treat male teens with specific disorders. By age fifteen, most boys have reached puberty. If a boy has not gone through puberty, he remains small in size and looks young. His voice has not deepened, and he has little body hair. Because of this, some of these teens may develop social problems. For example, although they once enjoyed sports, they no longer can play against teen boys whose testosterone levels have increased, and so are taller and stronger. So, doctors may treat these teens with a small amount of a testosterone-like drug for some months. These boys are constantly monitored to make sure they are growing properly and no bone damage is occurring.

For both boys and girls who are too short, doctors may prescribe two hormones, anabolic steroids and growth hormone. This combination can bring about improvement in the growth rate of very short teens.

From the 1930s to the late 1970s, doctors prescribed anabolic steroids to treat depression. These drugs proved quite useful, but they fell out of favor with doctors as other more effective drugs were developed and used. In current experiments, researchers have used anabolic steroids in three new ways: to treat osteoporosis, a condition where bone loss occurs; to treat low sexual desire; and as a male birth-control pill.

Another use for anabolic steroids is to counteract the effects of lower testosterone production in healthy adult men who are growing older. Some researchers have found that testosterone may help restore muscles and bones in aging men. Testosterone may also help improve older men's mood, thinking, and sex drive.

Sometimes high doses of anabolic steroids are given to women who want to become males. However, this is not an officially approved medical use in the United States, and other drugs are used instead.[6]

Veterinary Uses for Steroids

Veterinarians use anabolic steroids to treat animals. Various steroids are approved for use in cattle, horses, cats, and dogs. A few studies have shown that these drugs stimulate an animal to gain weight. When cattle are given testosterone pellets, for example, their weight increases. This helps increase meat production. Steroids also improve an animal's coat and mood.

Nonsteroid Substitutes and Steroidal Supplements

Many different types of nonsteroid drugs are found within the illegal anabolic steroid market. Like anabolic steroids, they are sold similarly and treated the same way. These substances are mainly used as an alternative to anabolic steroids. Examples include clenbuterol, human growth hormone, ephedra, insulin, insulin-like growth factor, and GHB.

Since the 1990s, a number of steroidal supplements, either testosterone or nandrolone, have been marketed in the United States. Steroidal supplements, also known as prohormones or prosteroids, are not the same as anabolic steroids, but they supposedly have anabolic effects, causing bigger muscles. Steroidal supplements

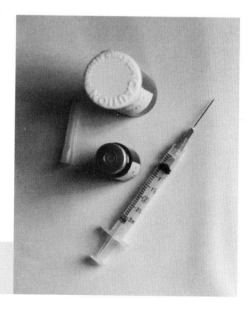

Anabolic steroids can be taken orally or by injection.

such as dehydroepian-drosterone (DHEA) and androstenedione (street name andro) are used by the body to make testosterone and estrogen. In the United States, both DHEA and andro can be bought legally without a prescription. Many commercial stores, including health food stores, carry DHEA and andro as well as other steroidal supplements. Steroidal supplements are also available through the Internet and at gyms and health clubs.

Steroidal supplements are often referred to as dietary supplements. However, they are not food products. Like anabolic steroids, steroidal supplements are banned by the National Football League (NFL), National Collegiate Athletic Association, and International Olympic Committee. The Food and Drug Administration (FDA) does not regulate steroidal supplements, and these substances are not held to the same strict standards as drugs.

Here is a list of some andro products legally sold in the United States:

- 1-AD (Androstenediol)
- 3-Andro Xtreme
- Andro-Gen
- Andro-Stack
- Androstat
- Animal Stak
- Nor Andro Ripped Fuel Stack
- Nor-Stak
- Nor-Tek

Scientists have not conducted many studies on steroidal supplements such as DHEA and andro. They do not yet know exactly how andro and other steroidal supplements work, nor do they know with certainty if they provide benefits or side effects.

East German researchers developed androstenedione in the 1970s. They used this substance to try to improve the performance of their Olympic swimmers and other athletes. By the mid-1990s, andro had hit the United States market, but sales were slow. That changed in 1998 when steroidal supplements jumped into the media spotlight. That year, St. Louis Cardinals baseball player Mark McGwire successfully broke Roger Maris's home-run record by hitting seventy home runs. He told news reporters that he used the steroidal supplement androstenedione. After that, an andro craze developed in the United States.

Androstenedione is found in meat and some plants. Users take the artificial substance in large quantities. For example, advertisements say that a 100-milligram dose of androstenedione increases testosterone by up to 300 percent for nearly three hours.[7]

A spokesperson, an endocrinologist (a scientist who studies and treats the endocrine system) at the famed Mayo Clinic in Rochester, Minnesota, said, "There's not even an answer to the question, 'What does it do?' There just isn't enough good published research to back up the claims that if you take andro, you'll see a 300 percent increase in testosterone levels."[8]

Researchers know little about the side effects of

steroidal supplements. If large quantities of these substances greatly increase testosterone levels in the body, then they are likely to produce the same side effects as anabolic steroids. As a result, labels on many andro products say that the substance should NOT be used by women, teens, or people with any medical conditions, including diabetes and heart disease.

The Association of Professional Team Physicians recommends that androstenedione be banned from all competitive sports. This association is made up of doctors from professional sports teams. According to these doctors, andro has a chemical structure similar to anabolic steroids. As a result, this drug may cause serious health problems, similar to those caused by anabolic steroids. Some stores are being careful. For example, the national chain General Nutrition Centers has banned the sale of andro in its thousands of stores across the country.[9]

DHEA has been sold over-the-counter as a dietary supplement in the United States since 1994. However, the International Olympic Committee, many American sports organizations, and some countries have banned it.

3

Who Is Using?

Athletes have been using anabolic steroids since the 1950s. During the following two decades, professional athletes were the main users of these drugs. But by the 1980s, illegal use of steroids had sky-rocketed among adults, teens, and even children in elementary grades. For example, in published surveys, middle school students have reported that steroids were available at their schools.[1]

Reasonably accurate counts of steroid users in the United States were not made until the late 1980s. Up until then, no one knew the extent of steroid abuse across this country.

Just how reliable these statistics are is at issue. No one knows how honest people are when reporting steroid drug use. That is because steroid use is illegal for performance enhancement, which may make some people afraid to be truthful about their steroid use. Some people may not remember previous drug use, perhaps because they have chosen to forget their actions. College or professional athletes may not be honest for fear of losing their scholarships or jobs and income. Others may not tell the truth for fear of tarnishing their sports records.

Teen Counts

The first published survey of teen use of steroids was in 1975. That year, researchers asked students in ten Arizona high schools about their use of anabolic steroids. Four percent of high school athletes reported anabolic use, and less than one percent of all high school students said they used steroids.[2]

Several other studies in the mid-1980s showed similar results. In 1988, the *Journal of the American Medical Association* reported the results of the first national study of steroid use. In this large study, 3,403 male twelfth graders in forty-six schools across the United States were asked about their use of anabolic steroids. The researchers found that 6.6 percent of those surveyed—or one in fifteen—said that they had used or were using anabolic steroids.[3] So, at that time, about 500,000 male teens were estimated to have had experience with anabolic steroids.

The researchers also reported that two thirds, or 66 percent, of teens had started using steroids at age sixteen or younger.[4] This study clearly showed that elite athletes were not the only ones taking anabolic steroids.

In 1993, another large study was reported in the *New England Journal of Medicine*. Nearly 1,900 high school students in Georgia were asked about their drug use. Similar to the 1988 results, 6.5 percent of teen males said they had used anabolic steroids without a doctor's prescription.[5]

Many more local and state studies have been carried out since 1988. In addition, various ongoing national surveys have been conducted on steroid use among teenagers. The Monitoring the Future Study (MTF) is a national survey that has been conducted each year since 1975. The University of Michigan's Institute for Social Research conducts the MTF studies with funding from the National Institute on Drug Abuse (NIDA). Some 45,000 to 50,000 eighth, tenth, and twelfth graders are surveyed each year for the MTF. Researchers determine how many teens are using steroids and other drugs. They also examine drug-related attitudes and beliefs of drug users.

According to the MTF:

- In 1998, 2 percent of tenth graders reported an increase in lifetime use of steroids. That figure jumped to 2.7 percent in 1999.

- 68 percent of seniors understood the risks associated with steroids. A year later, 62 percent reported perceived risks.

- For twelfth graders in 1999, 3.1 percent of males and 0.6 percent of females reported steroid use. In 2000, 2.5 percent of males and 0.9 percent of females reported they used steroids.[6]

What do all these numbers from these various studies mean? When analyzed together, these local, state, and national studies show that:

- Four percent of high school seniors abused steroids at least once.[7]

- In addition, 2.4 percent of female high school students have used anabolic steroids.[8]

- More than one million people have used illegal steroids, and about half are teens.[9]

- The number of male teens who have used steroids has been rapidly increasing since 1988.[10]

- Steroid use is higher among males than females. This includes a higher level of steroid use over a lifetime.[11]

- About three times as many male teens use steroids compared with female teen users.[12]

- Steroid abuse is growing most rapidly among young women.[13] According to a Penn State University study, about 175,000 girls use anabolic steroids.[14]

- More than half the teens who use steroids started before age sixteen. Some users start as young as age ten.[15]

Female teens, in their quest for a particular body type, sometimes turn to steroids to help them achieve their goal. Others, like this girl, embrace a healthy lifestyle instead.

No one yet has an accurate count of teen steroid abuse in the United States. It is difficult to track the exact numbers, since the use of steroids in sports is illegal. The numbers vary. The Healthy Competition Foundation recently reported these two statistics:

- Five percent of young people from ages twelve to seventeen took anabolic steroids or steroidal supplements. That translates into one million teens.

- About 390,000 young people between the ages of ten and fourteen took anabolic steroids or steroidal supplements.[16]

All these studies also show that steroid use is not limited to any one group of teens. Teens have reported steroid use in all types of schools. Teens from rich, middle-class, and poor families use them. Young people of various races, whether they live in cities, towns, or rural communities, use them.

"You see anyone in high school who is big—has ripped mass [large, rippling muscles], the curl in the biceps, the veins—and you know he's on it. He is juiced [taking steroids]," said one teen steroid user.[17]

Males make up the majority of teen users. However, more and more females, especially teen athletes, are using steroids to gain muscle. Use of steroids is especially high among female teen athletes in track and field, soccer, basketball, volleyball, and school dance and drill teams.

The 2001 MTF study also showed that steroids are readily available to teens. Forty-four percent of twelfth graders reported that it was "fairly easy" or "very easy" to get steroids. Among tenth graders, 33 percent recorded this response. Twenty-three percent of eighth graders reported the same responses.[18]

Teen anabolic steroid abuse occurs in countries outside the United States. Canada, England, Sweden, South Africa, and Australia have reported teen steroid use. These countries have rates of teenage use similar to those in the United States.

Who Is Using in Sports?

The spread of steroids for both male and female athletes has followed a similar path. Strength athletes such as weight lifters were the first group of athletes to use these substances. Track-and-field athletes were the next users. Steroid use then spread into basketball, swimming, gymnastics, lacrosse, softball, and football. By the late 1970s, Pat Donovan, an offensive lineman with the Dallas Cowboys from 1975 to 1983, said, "Anabolic steroids are very, very accepted in the NFL."[19]

Until the 1970s, researchers did not investigate steroid abuse. The information then gathered was based on stories or rumors talked about by sports figures or captured by the news media. Teen use of steroids in sports was reported as early as 1959.

Since the 1970s, the United States Congress has held hearings on the issue of performance-enhancing drugs used in sports. During these hearings, various people testified as to the extent of steroid abuse by athletes. Current and former athletes spoke, as well as some coaches and sport federation officials. At each of these hearings, all speakers agreed that a serious steroid-abuse problem exists.

Surveys of sports steroid users yield various counts. Athletes in the 1972 Olympic Games reported that about two thirds had used steroids at sometime.[20]

Drug testing of athletes seems to show a somewhat different count. During the 1990s, less than 3 percent of athletes in the National Collegiate Athletic Association, Olympics, and National Football League who were tested came up positive for banned substances.[21] This percentage seems low and is probably because drug users can often figure out ways to beat the drug tests. For example, they can stop using steroids before testing so that the test for drugs comes out negative. Just how much waiting before drug testing varies from user to user and depends on the number, type, and length of time steroids were used. Another issue is that no effective tests exist for some steroids. Yet these tests have caught a number of steroid users, both male and female, at major sporting events.

College Athletes

College athlete steroid use is increasing. In 1970, 15 percent of college athletes used steroids and by 1984, that figure jumped by 5 percent.[22] The researchers did not report rates separately for males and females, nor for specific sports.

In 1985, another study by two researchers surveyed over two thousand college athletes. There they found that 8.4 percent of football players said they had used steroids in the past twelve months. This was higher than the level of steroid use in any other sport. Track-and-field athletes reported 4 percent prior use. Other sports with steroid use were baseball (3.5 percent), basketball (3.6 percent), and tennis (3.6 percent). Steroid use was reported for only one women's sport—swimming; nearly one percent of female swimmers reported using steroids.[23]

The 1985 study was repeated during the 1988–1989 academic year. This time, data was collected from even more male and female athletes at eleven colleges and universities. The researchers found that steroid use had increased only slightly since 1985.[24]

The researchers repeated their study in 1993 with even more athletes. This time, they found some decrease in anabolic steroid use reported by males, but a significant increase among women athletes.

Another survey conducted by the NCAA in 1997 of nearly 14,000 athletes showed about the same results as those in 1993. The 2001 survey conducted by the NCAA shows that more college athletes were using steroids than had been four years earlier.[25]

How Anabolic Steroids Are Used

The reasons why people take anabolic steroids differ from reasons given for taking other drugs of abuse such as alcohol, marijuana, or cocaine. Users of these drugs take them to feel relaxed, energized, or high. In addition, these drugs surge to the brain and cause immediate changes. However, steroid users take these drugs to increase muscle mass, shape physique, and boost an athlete's energy.

Steroids can be taken in different ways. They can be taken orally as tablets or capsules, by injection into muscles, or rubbed into the skin as a gel or cream. Oral steroids do not last very long in the body, so they must be taken every day.

Users can inject liquid steroids once every three or four days. The liquid is usually in oil form so that it stays in the muscle for longer periods of time compared to swallowing a tablet or capsule. The liver destroys

According to some players, steroids have been widely used in the National Football League. Unfortunately, some student athletes also use them.

some of the oral steroid. So, injectable steroids do not affect the liver as much as oral steroids. Doses taken by abusers can be up to ten to one hundred times more than the doses used to treat medical conditions.

Steroids are most often taken in a cycle. This means that a user will have between four and fourteen weeks of steroid use, followed by a period of reduction in use or abstinence (no steroid use). Some users follow a cycling regimen because they want to stop their steroid use in time to compete in a sport. They do not want steroids to be found in their urine if they are tested. Some heavy users can complete six or seven cycles in a year.

Additionally, cycle users tend to stack the drugs, using multiple drugs concurrently. They take two or more different anabolic steroids, mixing oral and/or injectable types. Sometimes they include compounds designed for veterinary use. Abusers say that the different steroids interact to produce an even greater effect on muscle size than if each drug was used individually and also decrease side effects. There is no scientific evidence that supports these claims.

Another method of steroid use is called pyramiding, which lasts six to twelve weeks. At the beginning, users start with low doses of the drugs. They then increase the number of drugs used at one time or the dose and frequency of one or more steroids. Some users use as many as six different types of steroids. When they reach a peak amount at mid-cycle, they start to taper the dose down by the end of the cycle.

The increase of steroid use varies with different

types of training. Bodybuilders and weight lifters tend to escalate their dose to a much higher level compared to long-distance runners and swimmers. This megadosing may produce faster results. As with cycling, no scientific proof exists to show that pyramiding has any more effect than just using one type of steroid at a time.

What is known, though, is that during the time people are off steroids, they lose weight and strength. Anabolic steroids mimic the bodybuilding effects of testosterone. Anabolic steroids do cause muscles to grow. Athletes who have used these drugs report increases in muscle mass and strength. Some people gain weight on steroids. Often, though, the gain is a result of water retention. So, the bodybuilding changes are not permanent once someone goes off anabolic steroids.

4

Health Consequences

Some of the effects of anabolic steroids, such as rapid weight gain and muscle mass, are easy to see. Some changes, though, may not be seen until it is too late. Some of these effects are not reversible. Yet some steroid users, especially teens, may not think about the health consequences of using steroids. Most steroid abusers have at least one negative side effect. It may be something rather minor like acne or going bald. More serious problems could be the development of heart or liver damage or disease. Reported deaths in steroid abusers have occurred from liver disease, cancer, heart attacks, strokes, and suicides.

Overview of Health Effects

Anabolic steroid abuse has been associated with a wide range of side effects. These range from some that are physically unattractive, such as acne and breast development in men, to others that are life threatening, such as heart attacks and liver damage. Most effects are reversible if the person stops taking the drugs. Some, however, are permanent.

Most data on the long-term effects of anabolic steroids on people come from case reports reported in the medical literature by doctors, not from long-term studies. Based on these case reports, the risk of life-threatening effects appears to be low, but this could be because doctors are not recognizing the connection between steroid abuse and health problems. Or doctors may be underreporting these problems, or they may not know that someone is using steroids or used them in the past.

One study on mice and steroids was recently reported by the National Institute on Drug Abuse. The researchers found that exposing male mice for one fifth of their life span to steroid doses comparable to those taken by human athletes caused a high percentage of premature deaths. Lyle Alzado, a former Los Angeles Raiders football player, used anabolic steroids for many years. Alzado started using anabolic steroids in 1969 and continued until his death in 1992. He claimed that he was addicted to them, and that his rare form of brain cancer developed from using these substances.[1]

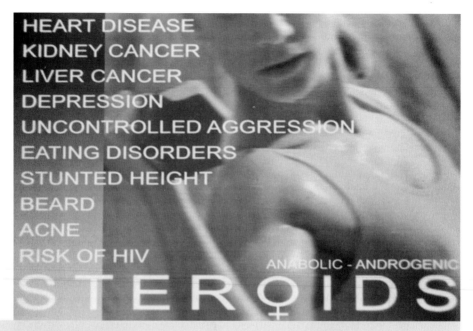

HEART DISEASE
KIDNEY CANCER
LIVER CANCER
DEPRESSION
UNCONTROLLED AGGRESSION
EATING DISORDERS
STUNTED HEIGHT
BEARD
ACNE
RISK OF HIV
ANABOLIC - ANDROGENIC
S T E R ♀ I D S

This poster lists some of the health effects of anabolic steroid use for women.

The Hormonal System

Steroid abuse disrupts the normal production of hormones in the body. This causes both reversible and irreversible changes. Many effects are reversible if the person stops taking steroids. However, some are permanent. Changes that can be reversed include reduced sperm production and shrinking of the testicles, which result in the male's becoming sterile (unable to have children).

Another effect of steroids is an enlarged prostate gland, which makes urinating difficult. Irreversible changes include male-pattern baldness and breast development. Enlarged breasts and painful lumps in the male breast can continue even after stopping steroids. Some men have had to have these lumps removed by surgery.

In the female body, anabolic steroids cause masculine traits to develop. A woman's shape may change to look more like a man's shape with a smaller bust and hips. Breast size and body fat shrink. The skin becomes coarse, the clitoris enlarges, and the voice deepens. Females may grow extra body hair on the chest and face, but they can lose their scalp hair and go bald. Their menstrual periods can become irregular, and they can become sterile. If steroids are continued for a long time, some of these effects are irreversible in females.

A reduced interest in sex occurs with long-term use of steroids in both males and females. Many males who take high doses of steroids become infertile during the time they use the steroids and remain infertile for some time after they stop. However, not all male and female steroid users become infertile, and not all steroids cause infertility.

Musculoskeletal System

Rising levels of testosterone and other sex hormones normally trigger the growth spurt that occurs during puberty. So, when these hormones reach certain levels, they signal the bones to stop growing. This locks a person into his or her maximum height. If a teen takes steroids, the artificially high sex hormone levels can signal the bones to stop growing sooner than they normally would have. The result is that these teens will not grow to their full height.

Anabolic steroids also make the tendons weak. Tendons connect muscles to bones. Weakened tendons cannot carry the extra weight that users put on and can tear or break down.

The Cardiovascular System

Steroid abuse can cause cardiovascular diseases, including heart attacks and strokes, even in people younger than age thirty. Steroids contribute to the development of cardiovascular disease. They do this, in part, by changing the levels of lipoproteins that carry cholesterol in the blood.

Steroids, especially the oral types, increase the level of low-density lipoprotein (LDL) and decrease the level of high-density lipoprotein (HDL). High LDL and low HDL levels increase the risk of arteriosclerosis, a condition in which fatty substances are deposited inside arteries and disrupt blood flow. If blood is prevented from reaching the heart, the person can have a heart attack. If blood is prevented from reaching the brain, a stroke can result.

Steroids also increase the risk that blood clots will form in blood vessels. When this happens, the blood flow is disrupted. This damages the heart muscle, causing it to not pump blood effectively. These drugs can cause an unhealthy enlargement and weakening of the pumping action of the heart.

Benji Ramirez, age seventeen, was a high school senior who played football for Ashtabula High School in

Ohio. During practice on Halloween, he collapsed. He died in a nearby hospital. Everyone was shocked that a young, healthy athlete could die so suddenly.

What killed him? The doctors said that it was steroids. From taking steroids for two years, Ramirez had caused serious damage to his body.

When doctors examined Ramirez, they found that his heart was diseased, his testicles had shrunk, and he had puncture wounds on his thighs. Friends reported that Ramirez wanted to be big and that the teen believed that "steroids were not harming him or that taking them was worth the risk."[2]

The Liver

The liver is the second-largest organ in the human body. It processes foods and some vitamins, filters unwanted material from the blood, destroys old, worn-out red blood cells, and produces bile, a digestive fluid. Bile helps digest fatty food when it reaches the intestines. The liver also breaks down and filters out drugs such as steroids.

The liver must work hard to handle steroids, especially steroids taken by mouth. Over time, the liver cannot keep up with high amounts of steroids. The liver becomes damaged. It reacts by releasing higher than normal amounts of bile into the bloodstream. Once bile starts to flow into the bloodstream instead of the intestines, the skin and whites of the eyes turn yellow. This condition is called jaundice. However, jaundice usually disappears after stopping steroid use.

Steroid abuse can cause liver tumors. Liver tumors seem to occur in one to three percent of people who take high doses of certain anabolic steroids for more than two years.[3] Some of the tumors are cancerous, while more than half of the tumors disappear when steroid use stops.

Steroids can also cause a rare and serious condition called peliosis hepatis. In this disease, small, blood-filled cysts form in the liver. Both the tumors and cysts sometimes can rupture. This causes internal bleeding and may result in death. Peliosis hepatis is not easily diagnosed by doctors, and people often have no symptoms in the beginning.

While a teen, Jorge began using steroids. He was a bodybuilder and worked out regularly. However, he was not satisfied with his progress and wanted to be bigger and stronger, so he took steroids. "In basically three to six months I went from being able to bench press 250 pounds once, and it was difficult doing it once, to doing 12 reps [repetitions] with 300 pounds easily."

Jorge developed serious liver problems from using steroids. He nearly died and stopped using them. Jorge now says that steroids are too risky. "I'm here to tell people and especially young people that yes, it can happen, and yes, it will happen to you."[4]

The Kidneys

The kidneys dispose of extra water and unwanted materials in the form of urine. The kidneys maintain the water balance in the body and the acidity (pH) of the blood. The kidneys also release the protein erythropoietin. Erythropoietin causes the bone marrow to increase the number of red blood cells that form in the bloodstream and release vitamin D. This vitamin stimulates the intestines to absorb calcium, which helps control blood pressure. The kidneys also eliminate drugs through urine.

As with the liver, steroids can damage the kidneys and cause them to work harder. Over time, the kidneys can stop working. A dialysis machine then takes over the kidney's function. The person has to be hooked up every day to this machine. Some people may get a kidney transplant from a donor. However, kidneys for transplants are difficult to get, and many people die waiting for a transplant.

The Prostate

As a result of taking long-term steroids, some men may be at greater risk for developing prostate cancer. This type of cancer is usually a disease of older men. However, it is the second leading cause of cancer death in American men. (Lung cancer is the first leading cause.) Typical treatment for prostate cancer is to reduce testosterone in the body. This is done by hormone therapy. These drugs block signals from the brain that tell the testicles and adrenal glands to stop making so much testosterone. These drugs are often combined with other treatments such as surgery (removal of the prostate gland), radiation, and chemotherapy. Some researchers predict that

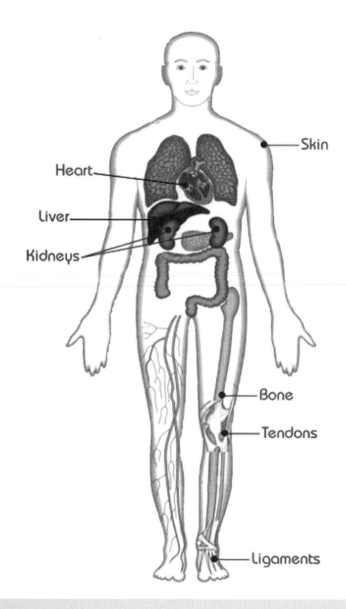

Skin

Heart

Liver

Kidneys

Bone

Tendons

Ligaments

Anabolic steroids can damage many of the body's organs, including those shown.

the steroid users of today will face a greater risk of prostate cancer as they age.

Cosmetic Effects

Steroid abuse can cause acne, cysts or whiteheads, oily hair, and oily skin. Acne and cysts can cause skin scarring. In men, larger breasts can develop. Some men can go bald from steroid abuse but will grow more body hair. These cosmetic effects are quite visible and may be very troublesome for abusers who are concerned about their appearance.

Consequences of Injection

Some abusers who inject anabolic steroids do not sterilize the injection site or use nonsterile needles. They may also share contaminated needles with other abusers. In addition, some steroids, both fake and real, are manufactured illegally in dirty conditions. Any of these factors puts abusers at risk to get life-threatening viral infections such as HIV, hepatitis B, and hepatitis C. The year 1984 marked a first: A shared needle was reported as the cause of a bodybuilder getting AIDS.[5] Other cases of AIDS have since been reported in steroid users due to needle sharing.

Abusers can also develop endocarditis. This bacterial illness causes potentially fatal inflammation of the inner lining of the heart. Bacterial infections can also cause pain and infection at injection sites.

Many brands of steroids must be injected with large syringes and needles that measure $1\frac{1}{2}$ inches or more. Users inject into the large muscle groups of the buttocks, thighs, or shoulders. Steroids are never injected into the veins. "The first time I tried to inject myself, I almost fainted, and one of my friends did faint," said one nineteen-year-old from Arizona. "Sometimes one of the guys will inject in one side of his butt one day and the other the next. Then we all laugh at him because he can barely sit down for the next three days."[6]

Another steroid injector said, "We all knew who was using. We exchanged information on new drugs that were on the market. We got our steroids through the gym owner. In fact, he would inject them for us, in the rear."[7]

Other Drug Use

Steroid users often take other drugs for three reasons: to manage the side effects of steroids, to increase the bodybuilding effects of steroids, or to avoid detection of steroids through urine testing. These drugs bring their own risks to users. Males, for example, might take estrogen blockers to keep their breasts from enlarging. Water pills or diuretics may be taken to dilute the urine before blood testing. Or they may be used to eliminate fluid retention, which helps make the muscles look more defined. Salt tablets and aspirin are also taken before workouts, to increase blood pressure and decrease the blood's thickness. Users say this produces an increased heart pumping effect.

Two hormones sometimes taken with steroids are human chorionic gonadotropin (HCG) and human growth hormone. HCG is an injectable hormone. It stimulates the testicles to produce more testosterone and to keep them from shrinking. Human growth hormone is taken to increase muscle and body size.

Recent research suggests that men who use anabolic steroids may begin to abuse heroin or other opioid drugs (drugs derived from opium), such as prescription pain relievers. In one study, researchers found that among 227 men admitted for treatment of opioid addiction, 21 (9.3 percent) reported that they had used anabolic steroids. None of the men had used other illegal drugs prior to their steroid abuse. Most of the men said they were introduced to opioids through the dealers who supplied them with steroids and through the bodybuilders they knew.

Why had these men used opioids? Eighteen said they used these drugs to counteract negative effects of steroids, including inability to sleep and irritability. Fourteen said they used opioids to counter the depression that developed when they stopped using steroids and went into withdrawal.[8] During withdrawal, the body tries to get used to not having the drug. Some people get very ill when they withdraw, or go off, some illegal drugs.

Pete's Story

Pete, a Massachusetts college junior, had been invited to try out for a national hockey team. Pete had plenty of talent, but he stood at 6'1" tall and weighed just 165 pounds. This put the promising hockey player on the light side for professional hockey. Pete decided to turn to anabolic steroids to bulk up and develop a more muscular body.

The steroids worked. Pete gained weight and increased his strength. However, the illegal drugs affected his muscles. His hand muscles felt tight, and he could barely grasp his hockey stick. He remembered, "The worst part was that I got so winded, they had to take me off the ice and have me breathe into a bag. I thought I was having a heart attack." Pete did not make the hockey team.

Next Pete tried a new sport, bodybuilding. He also upped his steroid amounts. Now, he said, "I could lift 425 pounds. My weight shot up to 242, and I had a 32-inch waist. I felt there was nothing I couldn't do." Pete worked at a local prison and thought he could break up any fight there.

The number of prison inmates in the fight did not matter to him, as he felt he could do it all. "I realize now how foolish that was," he admitted.

Pete talked like a fairly typical heavy steroid user. Many, like Pete, say they feel invincible when on these drugs. Pete explained, "It was an ego trip. People were constantly telling me how great I looked."[9] Pete quit steroids when blood showed up in his urine.

Behavioral Effects

Starting in the late 1980s, publications began to report that steroids can provoke manic symptoms, such as mood swings, aggression, euphoria (feeling high), larger-than-life ideas, reckless behavior, and decreased need for sleep. Medical literature, as well as newspapers and magazines, carried stories about violence committed by users on high levels of steroids. In surveys, steroid abusers reported that the drugs prompted them to acts of aggression.

Since the 1990s, some scientific studies have shown that steroids can alter the user's mood. These drugs cause some users to feel more aggressive and angry. In turn, users may take out these feelings on unsuspecting people. These intense, out-of-control bursts of anger are called "roid rage." "Roid rage" is a slang expression to describe the aggressive feelings, thoughts, and behaviors of anabolic steroid users.

In an extensive study in 2000, fifty men between the ages of twenty and fifty were observed for twelve weeks. Each man received weekly steroid injections and also underwent psychological tests. In addition, each man kept a daily diary of his psychological symptoms. Of the fifty men who received all of their steroid injections, forty-two had only minimal psychological reactions to the drug. However, two men developed serious manic symptoms. Another six developed moderate symptoms.

"People who responded to the steroid had different combinations of manic symptoms," reported the researchers. "One man had an aggressive outburst at work. Once, when he got cut off in traffic, he followed the person in his car for several miles. The other man with the marked reaction became euphoric and had a decreased need for sleep. Among the moderate responders, one man playing in a college sports competition found himself wanting to beat up his opponent. He

The aggressive behavior that can result from steroid use is known as "roid rage." Such bursts of rage can sometimes cause violent acts and destruction of property.

said that he had never had such aggressive feelings before."

The researchers also reported that in tests with computers, the "aggressive responders would pound on the board and yell and swear at what they thought was their opponent in the neighboring booth, who was, of course, a computer. It was quite dramatic."[10]

Based on this and other studies, the federal government has stated that some steroid abusers can develop aggressive behavior. The National Institute on Drug Abuse states, "Somewhere between 2 and 10 percent of men develop manic behavior and other neuropsychiatric complications from high doses of steroids."[11]

The effects of steroids on violent behavior vary widely and depend on the social situation and the person's characteristics. For example, one steroid user was cut off on a road by another driver. He went after the other driver, cornered him, and then smashed his windshield with a crowbar. Another user bought an old car, then drove it into a stone wall as a friend videotaped the destruction. Both men had never shown such violent behavior before they used steroids. Both returned to their original personalities after they stopped using steroids.[12]

A shy, quiet, withdrawn teen, age fourteen, began using steroids. At the same time, he started to have problems with the police for various small crimes. At age sixteen, he heard that his girlfriend had gone to a nearby town with another male teen. He began taking large amounts of testosterone and a second steroid at this time. After his girlfriend returned, he

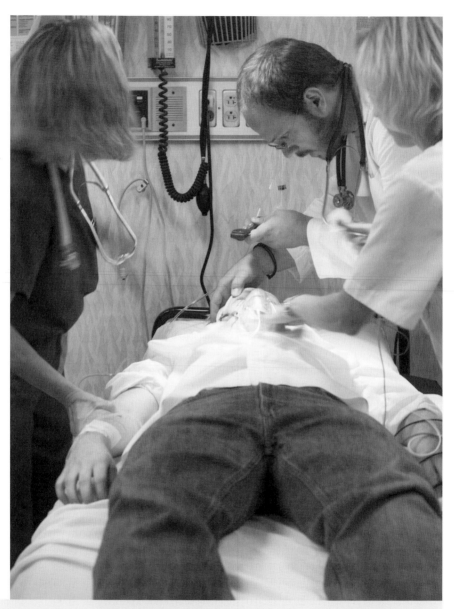

Steroid use can lead to medical emergencies and permanent physical damage.

drank some beers, then took her out to a wooded area. There he stabbed his girlfriend repeatedly with a carving knife from his mother's kitchen. This teen is in a state prison for life for killing his girlfriend. He can never get parole.[13]

Steroid Addiction

Withdrawal symptoms are the indication that steroids are addictive. Withdrawal means the uncomfortable effects users have when they stop taking steroids for a period of time. When users stop taking steroids, the body is left with an altered chemistry. The results include mood swings, feeling tired or restless, appetite loss, inability to sleep, reduced interest in sex, and depression. The depression can get so bad that it can lead to suicide thoughts and/or attempts. If left untreated, the depression can last a year or more after the abuser stops taking steroids.

Taylor Hooton, a popular seventeen-year-old in Plano, Texas, was expected to be a starter on his high school baseball team. He had begun using steroids a year earlier, and his personality changed. He became aggressive and irritable. He stole a digital computer, laptop computer, and money from his parents, and seriously beat up another teen. He lied to his parents about his drug use.

Taylor finally admitted to using steroids, and then stopped taking them. As he went through steroid withdrawal, Taylor became very depressed and killed himself.[14]

Users can become dependent on steroids.

Dependence develops when users cannot stop or decrease use, they take more drugs than they intend, or they continue use in spite of negative effects, tolerance, and withdrawal. Tolerance is when someone needs more of a drug to get the same effect at lower doses, or the user has diminished effects from the same dose. Steroid tolerance was first reported in animals in the 1950s. Two studies in 2000 showed that steroid abusers reported tolerance.[15]

Even when teens know many of the health risks involved, the temptation to use steroids can be strong. Sean Pitts of Murray, Utah, began using steroids to enhance his performance for baseball and football. Sean, age sixteen, said, "I got stronger and quicker than ever before."

He lied to his coaches and parents about his steroid use. "I didn't care about the consequences you hear about."

Less than a year later, Sean felt tired a lot and had bloody noses. He had trouble urinating and his skin became yellow. Sean finally told his parents. "My mom cried. My dad was really disappointed in me. It was awful. You lose trust."

Sean found out he had damaged his liver with steroid use. Luckily, once he stopped, his liver began to heal. Sean worked hard to build up his muscles and performance—without drugs. Now eighteen, he said, "I was happier than ever, because I had accomplished more than just succeeding at sports: I had overcome a terrible habit."[16]

5

Steroids and Body Image

Our society rewards people who look physically fit and attractive with many benefits and recognition. Some people see steroids as a means to those benefits. They aim to create a beautiful body, by sculpting and building it, so they take steroids to increase their muscle size or reduce their body fat. Sometimes these people are bodybuilders, models, actors, or dancers. They use their bodies to get admiration and money. Some teens fall into this category when they use steroids.

Some people who abuse steroids have experienced physical or sexual abuse. They may try to increase their muscle size to protect themselves. Some teens take steroids as part of a pattern of high-risk behaviors. These teens take other risks, too, such as drinking and driving.

Other people take steroids to enhance their ability to fight or to intimidate others with their muscular bodies. They include bodyguards, security guards, prison guards, police, soldiers, bouncers, and gang members. These people use their bodies to intimidate, frighten, or to fight others.

Striving for More Muscles

Tom (not his real name) liked the way steroids made his body look. When Tom broke his leg, he began weight training to keep fit. His new muscles delighted him, but the teen admitted, "I wanted more size, faster." Encouraged by his personal trainer, Tom started to take steroids one summer. He took two types, one as pills and one by injections into his buttock muscles.

When school started in September, Tom's new look brought him instant attention. "I got a huge response from guys and girls. I was sort of shocked at first, but after a while, I began to like it." However, when he stopped using steroids, he lost weight rapidly and got depressed.

To counter these effects, Tom bought more steroids and started another cycle. Finally he stopped taking steroids because he developed a serious shoulder injury that forced him to stop working out. Tom, now nineteen, said, "If I hadn't had the injury, I would probably still be taking them now. But that could just as easily have kept heading me down the road to self-destruction."

Tom said that using steroids to develop a muscular body is a reaction to a body-image obsession in American society. "Kids see the well-built guys on TV, getting the girls and the respect from the guys, and they want that, too."[1]

Tom is right. Growing numbers of teen boys and girls use drugs to build muscle, lose fat, or improve their appearance. Steroids are probably the best known body-image drugs. Currently, researchers do not know how many teens take steroids for body image, but some believe that number could be high.[2]

Research on competitive and noncompetitive bodybuilders shows three motivators for using steroids for both groups of people: wanting to excel at competitive bodybuilding; wanting to be more muscular; and gaining increased confidence when more muscular. Many of these users also had a lack of concern or belief in side effects of steroids.[3]

Michael (no last name given), age thirty-two, said that at age fourteen, he started working out, turning to muscle magazines for advice. Although he strove for the bodies he saw in these magazines and at his gym, he could not reach his goal. So he turned to steroids to bulk up. He knew the risks, but felt his looks were more important.[4]

Pressure to Have an Ideal Body

Why has there been an increase in body-image drug use since the 1980s? American society has placed

Obsession with body image in this country has led to an increase in steroid use as well as exercising in hopes of achieving an impossible ideal.

more and more pressure on both males and females to achieve an ideal body appearance. A number of studies point to this trend. Researchers are increasingly showing that our society puts pressure on people to attain a specific body image, one of low body fat, a lean appearance, and—at least for men— big muscles.

One body image study looked at Barbie, a popular girl's doll. With her large breasts, tiny waist, and extremely long, slender legs, Barbie has been said to contribute to the "thin is beautiful" look that is prevalent today in the movies, television, and ads.

Boys' action toys such as GI Joe have become bigger and more muscular over the years. They look like bodybuilders on steroids, with massive necks and bulging arm and chest muscles.

Since its introduction in 1964, GI Joe is probably the most famous and longest running of American action toys. The original GI Joe corresponded to a man of average height and build. In 1982, the action toy still looked like an average man. By 1992, GI Joe had grown taller and more muscular, particularly in the chest. Just a few years later, by the mid-1990s, the same action figure became massively muscular. His arms rippled with muscles. His biceps were nearly the same size as his waist.

Other action toys have undergone the same transformation, including the Star Wars characters, the Gold Ranger, Iron Man, Batman, and the Wolverine. For example, in 2000, the Batman action figure had measurements that—in a grown man— would correspond to a 30-inch waist, 57-inch chest, and 27-inch biceps. Such measurements are nearly impossible to obtain unless steroids are used.

Many children play with Barbie and action toys. They absorb the message of how females and males should supposedly look. The sale of toys such as GI Joe and Batman is over one billion dollars a year.[5]

What this means is that both males and females "get treated as objects, that they internalize this, and that it damages their self-esteem," said Kelly D. Brownell. Brownell is the director of the Yale Center for Eating and Weight Disorders. "More and more, guys are falling into the same thing [as females]. They're getting judged by how they look."[6]

For some male teens, the incentive for bigger muscles sometimes comes from girls. "For a lot of them, steroids are something that builds their confidence. At that age, they're considering getting into sexual relationships that are kind of scary. Changing their appearance so they feel more attractive can make it easier," said Dr. Aynsley Smith.[7]

The more muscles, the more dates seem to result, claim some teens. A drug expert at the United States Food and Drug Administration said, "Bulging muscles are in. Guys want to look good at the beach. High-school kids think steroids may enhance their ability to get an athletic scholarship, play pro sports or win the girl of their heart."[8]

Alexander Bregstein, a teen, said that when he took steroids, lifted weights, and worked out regularly, his social life improved. With his increased muscles and lean appearance, he got more dates and more attention from girls. He said, "But in a way it depresses me, that I had to do this for people to get to know me."[9] However, studies have shown that while men think women prefer men with lots of muscle, most women find big muscles unattractive. Researchers have found that most women prefer a more average physique.[10]

More Brainwashing

Body-image brainwashing continues in other ways. Teens, as well as those in other age groups, are watching more and more professional wrestling. The World Wrestling Federation (WWF) began to sell out arenas with big, muscled stars in the mid-1980s. The public flocked to watch their favorite characters pretend to beat each other up. In the early 1990s, Vince McMahon, Jr., the owner of WWF, was arrested for supplying his stars with steroids.

Hulk Hogan, a WWF star, testified at McMahon's trial and admitted that he had taken steroids for thirteen years. He said he would pick up the drugs along with his paycheck at the WWF headquarters. Despite this testimony, McMahon was acquitted, or found not guilty, of steroid charges.

In 2002, the WWF became World Wrestling Entertainment (WWE). Today, the organization still has sell-out events, and millions watch its television programs. Some examples of very muscular wrestlers who are popular include Triple-H, The Rock, Brock Lesnar, "Big Poppa Pump" Scott Stiener, and "Stone Cold" Steve Austin.

The Rock, who went from wrestling with WWE

to starring in feature films, wrote frankly in his autobiography about his former steroid use. "I was 18, and I was being completely idiotic about it," he said. "Then I realized I didn't care to be the biggest or even the strongest guy around."[11]

Beyond professional wrestling, teens see super-muscular men in fitness and health magazines, comic

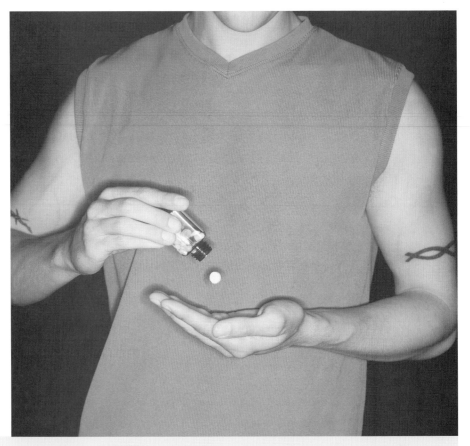

Some people take steroids in an effort to have a body type that few can achieve.

strips, television, and the movies. In recent years, the number of gymnasiums, health clubs, and other fitness facilities has grown rapidly. This health and fitness trend is not bad, of course, but unreal body-image expectations appear to be growing.

Surveys since 1973 show that both males and females in increasing numbers are unhappy with their bodies. In some body-image studies, researchers have found that many male teens chose a physical ideal that can only be attained by using steroids.

Here are more statistics that point to body-image dissatisfaction:

- About 50 million Americans begin a weight-loss diet each year.[12]

- Americans spend a whopping $33 billion on weight-loss products and services each year.[13]

- About 8 million people struggle with eating disorders each year.[14] Eating disorders are medical conditions that affect millions of people, mostly women and girls. The most common eating disorders among females are anorexia, or self-starvation, and bulimia, where the person overeats, then throws up food. Compulsive overeating, a condition that equally affects males and females, involves ingesting food long after the point of fullness.

- The number of men undergoing cosmetic surgery increased by about 34 percent between 1996 and 1998.[15]

According to researchers, these trends are tied to the growing numbers of males and females with body-image disorders. This includes eating disorders such as bulimia nervosa and anorexia nervosa. In bulimia nervosa, the person binges, or overeats, then vomits to get rid of excess food and calories. People with anorexia nervosa see themselves as fat, so they starve themselves. In reality, they grow thin and are undernourished. Another body-image disorder is muscle dysmorphia, in which a person has a distorted image of his or her muscle. People with this body-image disorder think they are nonmuscular, when they actually are muscled.

Kevin (no last name given) is in his early twenties and has muscle dysmorphia. He is a weight lifter and stands nearly six feet tall and weighs 230 pounds. Yet he is afraid that people think he is small, skinny, and nonmuscular.[16]

Patrick (no last name given) runs a store for weight lifters in a Boston suburb. He says that the saddest customers are the little boys, twelve and thirteen, brought in by young fathers. "The dad will say, 'How do we put some weight on this kid?' with the boy just staring at the floor. Dad is going to turn him into Hulk Hogan, even if it's against his will."[17]

6

Steroids and Sports

Sports have long held an important place in society. Many athletes are seen as heroes. Some earn a lot of money by entertaining the public. Other athletes in college and high school are a source of pride to the student bodies and their communities. Because sports are an important aspect of our society, drug use by athletes is a significant issue.

History

The recorded history of drugs used in sports stretches back many years. In 1865, some swimmers in canal races in Amsterdam,

69

Holland, were on various drugs.[1] What they were taking is not known. Prizefighters of the time drank alcohol, often brandy, during contests. They used strychnine, a poison, both as tablets and mixed into an ointment. They used this poison as an anesthetic, to dull pain. Written records show that they also took cocaine and heroin.[2]

Before motorized vehicles, bicycles were a main mode of transportation. Cycling races were popular in the 1800s, as were some of today's illegal drugs, such

Drug abuse in sports is not new. Bicycle racers in the 1800s sometimes used various dangerous drugs to give them energy.

as cocaine. Professional cyclists of that time period drank coffee boosted with extra caffeine and laced with cocaine or strychnine. Trainers would drop cocaine flakes onto cyclists' tongues as they pedaled by. When cyclists rested, trainers would massage cocaine mixed with cocoa butter into their legs. Other drugs were used, such as nitroglycerin, digitalis, or atropine (all three regulate the heart rate), and heroin and camphor.

After 1935, more and more synthetic forms of steroids were made. As early as the 1940s, body-builders may have begun using steroids to build muscle size and strength. Olympic stars began using these drugs in the 1950s. By 1956, anabolic steroid use was common among elite athletes. In 1956, Olympian Olga Fikotova Connolly said, "There is no way in the world a woman nowadays in the throwing events, at least the shot put and the discus, can break the record unless she is on steroids. These awful drugs have changed the complexion of track-and-field."[3]

Most of this early use went undetected. That is because the technology of drug testing did not allow reliable detection in the urine until the 1976 Olympic Games.

Even with the use of drug testing, anabolic steroid use has continued by Olympic competitors for decades. This trend seems to be growing, "I hear all the time from athletes that you can't compete internationally unless you use performance-enhancing drugs," said Dr. Robert Voy, former chief medical officer of the United States Olympic Committee and director of drug testing for the U.S. Olympic teams at the 1984 and 1988 games.[4]

Today, steroids are still an issue at the elite athlete level, such as professional sports and the Olympics, as well as in many other athletic sports. Some athletes use steroids in almost all sports. A White House-sponsored study in 1999 found that between 30 and 90 percent of athletes in some sports use performance-enhancing drugs.[5] Steroids have become prevalent in football, wrestling, track-and-field, swimming, and bodybuilding. Bodybuilders seem to be the number-one abusers. One bodybuilder said, "to appear in the Nationals [the National Bodybuilding Championship] without using steroids would be like competing in the Miss America Contest without makeup."[6] This bodybuilder ruined his chances of competing in the Nationals. Because of his steroid abuse, he cannot lift weights, he developed joint pain and weakness, and he permanently damaged his liver.

Steroids are having an increasing effect on professional baseball, the national sport of the United States. Baseball players talk openly about using steroids among themselves. Ken Caminiti, the National League's Most Valuable Player in 1996, went public with his steroid use in 2002. He had bought the drugs in Mexico. The baseball great said that using steroids improved his performance. However, he was using steroids so much, that his testicles shrank and his body nearly stopped producing its own testosterone. Caminiti estimates that "at least half the guys [in baseball] are using steroids. They talk about it. They joke about it with each other."[7]

Doctors think that steroid use is playing an important role in the increase in baseball injuries. This is especially true for severe injuries, such as complete muscle, tendon, and ligament tears. This also means players spend longer times out on disability, unable to play ball.[8]

In 2001, major league baseball instituted a drug policy for minor league players. The policy bans androstenedione, steroids, and other drugs of abuse. Players can be tested three times a year at any time. For each positive test, players can be punished with suspension and fined. In 2003, major league players began to be tested for steroid use, too.

Pressure to Perform

Steroids are banned by most major athletic organizations, including the International Olympic Committee, the National Football League, and the National Collegiate Athletic Association. However, some athletes looking for a competitive edge try to get away with using steroids. They try to hide it by stopping usage before an anticipated drug test. Or they may take masking drugs. These are drugs that hide the use of steroids.

Sport organizers around the world may ban the use of drugs known to enhance athletic performance, but some athletes will use them anyway. One of the main reasons people give for using steroids is to improve their performance in sports. Some athletes use steroids to get into college sports or onto professional sports teams. Once they have earned a place on the roster, players may find themselves under pressure to become even bigger and stronger. Steroids can help make gains in muscle size and strength more quickly than training alone does.

"I think part of it is that the coaches don't really want to know how the athletes can come back 30 pounds heavier a few months later," said Dr. Aynsley Smith of the Mayo Clinic's Sports Medicine Center in Rochester, Minnesota.[9]

In college, some players want to play professional sports. So they must improve their performance in training drills and in the weight room, as well as on the playing field. Some athletes may decide that the only way to meet the selection standards of the professional teams is to use steroids.

The problem of teen and young adult athletes and steroids is one not likely to go away. "The bottom line is that steroids are illegal and clearly can have life-threatening effects. Parents and coaches should realize that their athletes have probably at least considered using these supplements and should take measures to educate the athletes about what they may be getting into," said Smith.[10]

Another aspect to steroid use is the desire to win at any cost. Every two years since 1982, Dr. Bob Goldman, a doctor and an author, asks about two hundred athletes what they will do to gain a competitive edge. He asks assorted athletes, mostly Americans, these two questions:

"You are offered a banned performance-enhancing substance, with two guarantees: (1) You will not be caught. (2) You will win. Would you take the substance?" Nearly all say yes.

New rules about steroid use in baseball went into effect in 2003.

"You are offered a banned performance-enhancing substance that comes with two guarantees: (1) You will not be caught. (2) You will win every competition you enter for the next five years, and then you will die from the side effects of the substance. Would you take it?" More than half of the athletes say yes.[11]

Some athletes state other reasons why they use steroids. Some athletes reach a plateau at some point in their training. Banned drugs, they say, help them move beyond it. Another reason is that athletes make sacrifices to pursue their sport. When the effort does not yield the desired results, some may become frustrated enough to take banned drugs. Sometimes athletes are making good progress with their training, but they may become curious and take steroids to see what will happen.

One baseball player said, "Basically, steroids can jump you a level or two. The average player can become a star, and the star player can become a superstar, and the superstar? Forget it. He can do things we've never seen before."[12]

Doping in Sports: Steroids

Doping is the use of drugs that have been banned from competition. This includes anabolic steroids. One of the best known examples of doping occurred at the 1988 Summer Olympics in Seoul, South Korea. There, Canadian sprinter Ben Johnson set a world record in the 100-meter dash and won the gold medal—then lost it twenty-four hours later with a positive drug test for an anabolic steroid.

The International Olympic Committee issued a resolution against doping in 1962. It performed the first tests for banned drugs at the 1968 Winter Games in Grenoble, France, and at the Summer Games in Mexico City. At that time, the list of illegal substances was short and contained drugs such as amphetamines, stimulants that speed up the heart rate and breathing.

By the mid-1970s, the appearance of athletes in some sports was changing. For example, at the 1976 Olympics in Montreal, East German female swimmers showed markedly larger and more developed muscles than competitors from other countries. Athletes in field events such as the hammer throw and shot put were also much larger. By the end of the 1970s, the use of banned and soon-to-be-banned drugs was an accepted practice in track and field, weight lifting, swimming, rowing, cycling, and other events.

The IOC continued to identify substances that athletes were using to gain an advantage. At the same time, competitors and their coaches looked for drugs that could not be detected by drug testers. Through the 1980s and 1990s, drugs that promote muscle development and speed recovery from tough training sessions became popular in sports at the international, national, college, and high school levels.

In 1997, investigators of drug use in the Olympics stated that three types of athletes existed:

- The smallest group of athletes uses steroids and are caught.

- The next group of athletes do not use any banned steroids.

- The largest group of athletes take steroids but are not caught. They do this by taking drugs that are not tested for, using tested-for drugs below levels allowed by the IOC, or taking other substances to mask the steroids in their bodies when tests are run.[13]

The Olympics and Steroids

"Athletes are a walking laboratory, and the Olympics have become a proving ground for scientists, chemists, and unethical doctors. The testers know that the

[drug] gurus are smarter than they are. They know how to get under the radar," said Dr. Robert Voy.[14]

Today, both amateur and professional athletes use banned steroids. Steroid use tends to be most popular in sports that require great strength or endurance. Leading athletes have been disqualified in nearly all Olympic sports, including:

- In 1989, American sprinter Diane Williams testified at a Senate hearing that she had used oxandrolone (Oxandrin) and other anabolic steroids. Williams was a former United States national champion.

- German Dieter Baumann, the 1996 Olympic gold medalist in the 5,000-meter run, tested positive for the steroid nandrolone in 1999. He claimed that an unknown person added the steroid to his toothpaste so that he would test positive.

- In 1997, investigators in the former East Germany documented more than a hundred cases of steroid abuse in elite athletes. This doping was part of a national plan to train world champions.

- German marathon runner Uta Pippig was suspended from competition for two years after testing positive for testosterone in April 1998. Pippig won the New York Marathon in 1993 and the Boston Marathon in 1994, 1995, and 1996.

- The Festina cycle racing team admitted using anabolic steroids during the 1998 Tour de

France after a team support person was caught with the drugs. (Festina is a European company that makes watches. They sponsor a bicycle team for the Tour de France.) Six teams withdrew from the event after French authorities raided hotel rooms in search of banned substances.

- American shot-put star C. J. Hunter tested positive for nandrolone at the Bislett Games track meet and in three out-of-competition tests during the summer of 2000.

- More than a dozen athletes tested positive for banned substances at the 2000 Olympics in Sydney, including Armenian weight lifter Ashot Danielyan, Norwegian Greco-Roman wrestler Fritz Aanes, Latvian rower Andris Reinholds, and German freestyle wrestler Alexander Leipold for nandrolone. Russian sprinter Svetlana Pospelova tested positive for stanozolol.

- The United States Anti-Doping Agency announced some positive tests for banned substances during the first half of 2001. One athlete receiving citations was hurdler and 1992 Olympian Tony Dees, suspended two years for using nandrolone at the 2001 U.S. Indoor Track and Field Championships.

- In late 2001, Ludmilla Engquist, an Olympic gold-medalist hurdler in 1996 and part of Sweden's potential Olympic bobsled team, said she had taken anabolic steroids.

Female Athletes and Steroids

Investigators are not certain when women athletes began to use anabolic steroids. It may be that as early as the 1950s or 1960s, Soviet female track and field athletes were using them. In the mid-1960s, some of the female Eastern European Communist countries track and field athletes looked like males. As a result, they were given a chromosome test in 1967 at the European Cup.

A few athletes failed the chromosome test (meaning that they were men), and a few others quietly retired from competition before testing. The athletes who remained were indeed females, but the steroids they had been taking made their bodies look like men's.

During the 1970s, drug use was widespread among athletes in many Olympic sports, including cycling.

The spread of steroids in women athletes seems to have followed a similar path as male athletes. The strength athletes used the drugs first. Evidence of this comes from the 1968 Olympic Games in Mexico City by female throwers from Eastern European Communist countries.

By 1972, at the Munich Games, a few American female field athletes had been accused of using steroids. The evidence started to grow that female athletes were indeed using steroids. This information was based on government records, testimonials, and IOC drug-testing results. By the end of the 1970s, female sprinters, runners, swimmers, rowers, and some winter sport athletes were steroid users.

Today, this use has spread beyond the Olympics to college and high school use. In 1995, a fourteen-year-old girl tested positive for anabolic steroids. She was a female long jumper and sprinter and the world's youngest athlete to test positive.[15]

National Doping Programs

Since the 1960s, people have been suspicious that national doping programs existed in some countries. A national doping program is a program to give athletes drugs under the direction of or with the strong support of the country's government and sport federation officials. Doctors and scientists are also part of these programs.

Finally, in 1997, after many years of research, two investigators, Brigitte Berendonk and Werner Franke, reported that the German Democratic Republic (GDR) had run a national sport doping program for their country's athletes during the 1970s and 1980s. GDR called their secret program the "State Planning Theme 14.25." These two, and later other investigators, got their information from many secret scientific publications and from reports of doctors and scientists.

Hundreds of doctors and scientists performed research on athletes by giving them large doses of steroids. They also gave these athletes unapproved experimental drugs. Each year, several thousand athletes were given steroids, including female and male teen athletes. These teens were sometimes fourteen years old or younger. Many of these athletes were never informed of the program and were never told they were being given drugs. Many times, the athletes were told that their steroid pills or injections were vitamins or nutritional aids. However, "damaging side effects were recorded, some of which required surgical or medical intervention [treatment.]"[16] Such a state-sponsored program goes against the rules of sports. It also violates scientific and medical ethics. The consequences of such unethical testing have been huge. Many of these athletes, "achieved near-miraculous success in international competition, including the Olympics. But for most, their physical and emotional health was permanently shattered."[17]

Brigitte Berendonk, a former GDR Olympic track and field star, said, "The GDR athletic system, it was all a big scam. . . . The GDR, the system that I escaped from, had created monsters. These were not real people, just engineered experiments." Berendonk added, "We [the doped athletes] never talked about our bodies and the chemical changes. No one ever spoke; it was taboo. We never mentioned the dirty word of drug or steroid."[18] Berendonk later defected to West Germany.

Some of the coaches and doctors involved in this doping program have been brought to trial for their crimes. On March 18, 1998, the first German sports doping trial began. In August 2000, over four hundred doctors, coaches, and trainers from the former East Germany were found guilty of giving steroids to teens without their permission.[19] Some lost their license to practice medicine, and some went to jail.

In the meantime, German doctors and researchers have taken their doping knowledge to other countries. For example, the United States Justice Department's Drug Enforcement Agency (DEA) discovered that a drug developed and used in the GDR's doping program, androstenedione, or andro, has gained great popularity in the United States. This drug has been banned by the OIC, National Football League, the National Basketball Association, and the National Collegiate Athletic Association. Yet it is still accepted as a dietary supplement by major-league baseball and can be bought legally in America. Andro appears to have been exported from GDR to the United States and is now a $500 million industry in this country.[20]

Drug Testing

Drug testing is used to identify athletes who use banned drugs to enhance their sports performance. It is the most common method to determine if athletes are using anabolic steroids. Drug testing is now part of the Olympics, professional sports, college sports, and high school sports.

Many sports organizations are keenly aware of their public image. Their athletes are role models for young people and they need to maintain a clean, healthy image of their athletes. So, most professional and college athletic associations have adopted drug policies on the use of illegal drugs by their athletes.

Michael Mooney is a California bodybuilder and an authority on steroids. He designs steroid treatments for doctors to use for their AIDS patients. Mooney said, "I would say that nearly every top-level athlete is on something. The number of supposed steroid-free athletes—very well known athletes—who have contacted me about how to pass [drug] tests in just the last year blows my mind."[21]

Drug testing is a complicated process. When anabolic steroids are taken into the body, they are broken down and altered. Drug testing looks for the by-products of steroids that are produced in very small amounts. There are many steroids available and they vary from country to country. Sometimes drugs available in other countries are not used in the United States.

Drug testing is fraught with issues. No tests are available for some drugs, so there is no chance of getting caught, which is why some athletes will use banned drugs. Further, drug testing is expensive. Few sport organizations can afford to test more than a tiny sample of all competitive athletes. This means that the odds of being tested are not high unless an athlete wins at the national level.

Steroid users can often test clean if they know when the drug test is to be held. To do this, they stop taking the drugs long enough for the steroid to clear their bodies. Some steroids only last thirty-six hours in the body, while others take several months to clear the body. Drug testing is costly, about $120 per test.[22] This costs too much for most school systems. Also, the testing staff must be highly trained and able to do very detailed, careful laboratory work. The materials and instruments needed for drug testing cost a lot.

What fluid to test is another issue. Urine is the most common testing fluid. Steroid by-products can be detected in urine by several laboratory tests. Some athletes object to the loss of privacy when a stranger must watch them urinate. Drugs can also be detected in blood, hair, and saliva.

Blood testing presents a problem. For blood testing, the skin must be punctured and blood drawn. This can cause an infection to develop. Hair can be tested for drugs, but hair samples have no time line. So the steroid use may have occurred much earlier than the date of the test. Currently, saliva drug-testing results are unpredictable.

Another issue is whether drug testing goes against the Fourth Amendment. Do school, college, and professional sports teams have the right to force an athlete to undergo drug testing when there is no specific cause for drug-use suspicion? Athletes and others have hotly debated this issue.

Anti-Doping Agencies

The United States Anti-Doping Agency (USADA) is responsible for coordinating drug testing of American athletes. It conducts both in-competition tests, or tests at events such as the United States National Swimming Championships, and out-of-competition (OOC) tests. OOC tests are also called No Advance Notice tests.

OOC tests may be given to any athlete who is a member of a national sport governing body. Athletes must give this agency their current address and update the information if they move or go somewhere

Athletes such as this Canadian weight lifter are subject to testing for various kinds of drugs, including steroids.

else to train. When a representative of the USADA goes to an athlete's residence, the athlete must provide a sample for testing. If an athlete is not available for testing, the absence is reported and he or she is asked to provide an explanation. An athlete who misses three OOC tests in eighteen months may be ruled ineligible to compete for two years.

The World Anti-Doping Agency can only make recommendations to the International Olympic Committee. It cannot directly take action against athletes who test positive for banned drugs.

A New Drug

In October 2003, the USADA first learned about tetrahydrogestrineone (THG). THG is an anabolic steroid specially designed to be undetectable. However, the agency was able to develop a test for THG. Over four hundred samples from the 2003 World Championships in Paris were reanalyzed using the new test. Two athletes tested positive for THG: Britain's European 100 meters champion Dwain Chambers and United States shot putter Kevin Toth. Athletes testing positive for banned drugs, including steroids, are usually disqualified.

7

Laws

Both federal and state governments have laws to control anabolic steroid abuse. In 1988, Congress passed the Anti-Drug Abuse Act. This law made distributing or possessing steroids for nonmedical use a federal crime. A person could receive criminal penalties if caught.

During the 1980s, the media reported more and more stories about athletes using steroids in sports and a growing use of steroids by teens in high school. The United States government reacted by holding Congressional hearings between 1988 and 1990. The goal of these hearings was for Congress to determine if the Controlled

Substances Abuse Act should be amended to include anabolic steroids. At that time, this law covered drugs like cocaine, heroin, and LSD.

Congress listened to many experts and members of the public about steroid use and consequences. Experts included doctors and representatives from the FDA and the National Institute on Drug Abuse. Representatives from amateur and professional athletes and associations also testified.

Congress focused on three major issues: (1) concerns over a growing illicit market, (2) abuse by teens, and (3) the harmful long-term effects of steroid use. These three issues led Congress in 1990 to place anabolic steroids as a class of drugs into Schedule III of the Controlled Substances Act (CSA). The CSA defines anabolic steroids as any drug or hormonal substance chemically and pharmacologically related to testosterone (other than estrogens, progestins, and corticosteroids) that promotes muscle growth.

Called the Anabolic Steroid Act of 1990, the law went into effect on February 21, 1991. The Anabolic Steroid Act classified twenty-seven steroids as Schedule III substances. Under this law, the Drug Enforcement Agency regulates anabolic steroids. Since 1991, street prices of anabolic steroids have increased substantially as a result of this law. That is because demand has increased, and users are willing to pay the sharply inflated prices of illegal steroids.

Under the CSA, steroids are classified as Schedule III drugs. This is the same legal class for drugs such as amphetamines, methamphetamines, opium, and morphine. It is a federal crime to make, possess, or sell anabolic steroids for nonmedical uses. This law applies in all states.

The first time people are caught making or selling steroids illegally, they can get up to five years in prison and a two-year probation. In addition, they can be fined up to fifteen thousand dollars.

If caught a second or subsequent time making or selling steroids, people can get up to ten years in prison and two years' mandatory probation. This time, the fine jumps to thirty thousand dollars.

If someone possesses steroids, the punishment is up to one year in prison with a minimum fine of a

Use of anabolic steroids has been increasing in many sports, including basketball, and among both male and female athletes. Governments have responded with stricter laws and efforts to curb the manufacture, importation, and sale of these substances.

thousand dollars. If someone already has one drug crime record, he or she will go to prison for fifteen days or up to two years, with a minimum fine of twenty-five hundred dollars. The penalties are stiffer if the person has two or more drug crime records; he or she can go to prison for ninety days or up to three years, with a minimum five thousand dollar fine.

State Laws

During 1989 and 1990, many states classified anabolic steroids as controlled substances. During these years, at least twenty-two states tightened their control over these drugs.

The states differ as to how they classify anabolic steroids. This means a wide range of penalties exists if a person is caught illegally possessing, making, or selling these drugs. States also have different approaches to controlling steroids. Some states require that posters of the dangers of steroids be shown to the public. Other states have rules requiring that doctors be warned against prescribing steroids for nonmedical use.

New York has a higher standard than the federal government for steroids. This state classifies anabolic steroids as Schedule II controlled substances. If caught once with steroids, a person can go to jail for up to one year. For the sale of any amount of steroids in New York, a person can be jailed for up to seven years. He may also be placed on five years' probation and lose his license to drive a car or own a gun. The person will always have a felony drug sale on his record.

Other Consequences of the 1990 Law

Because of the Anabolic Steroid Act of 1990, drug companies have to keep very detailed records of the steroids they make and how much they sell. This is a very tight level of control. It is the same standard used for other commonly abused drugs, including drugs with codeine, an addictive narcotic.

Some scientists and lawmakers find this law difficult to deal with. It makes doing research on these drugs tougher, whether the research is done on people or animals. Most of our knowledge about steroids comes from research on animals.

Worldwide Problem

Most steroids do not come from the United States. Legal steroid sales in America have decreased since the 1990s. The lack of international control over sources of supply makes it difficult to attack the selling and distribution of steroids at their source.

The demand for illegal steroids has been supplied by countries such as Greece, India, Poland, Spain, and South Korea, according to the DEA. Recent DEA reporting indicates that in particular, people from Russia, Romania, and Greece are significant traffickers of steroids and are responsible for substantial shipments of steroids entering the United States.

Illegal steroid labs have sprung up in Eastern Europe since the mid-1990s. Political unrest in that area has allowed these labs to grow. Since Eastern Europe now supports private industry instead of communism, many rigid controls of the communist government have disappeared. As a result, drug traders there have flourished.

Europe, which includes Eastern Europe and the former Soviet Union, is a major sources for steroids. Some steroids coming from Canada are actually manufactured in Europe. Russia has reported that steroids reach its black market straight from its factories and warehouses. There these drugs are openly sold on the streets. In the past, the former Red Army had stored large quantities of steroids, which were given regularly to their soldiers to help them get bigger. That excess has disappeared illegally since the fall of communism because much was stolen out of the warehouses. In Bulgaria, veterinary steroids dangerous to humans have moved onto the black market. A police officer in the Czech Republic said, "It is quite easy to convert these products for human consumption."[1]

A huge raid in Britain shows the international nature of the business. In December 1993, the police raided two large buildings north of London. They had been told that an illegal laboratory was producing the designer drug ecstasy. Designer drugs are man-made variations of amphetamine, a stimulant of the central nervous system. However, the raid produced $1.6 million worth of drug equipment and raw testosterone. The testosterone had been obtained from a French pharmaceutical company.

The person in charge of the illegal steroid lab, along with a friend, was one step ahead of the British police. The two fled back to Australia, their native country. One year later, police stormed the friend's illegal steroid plant in Scotland. They collected $852,000 worth of steroids.

This whole operation was well designed. The two friends had professional machines turn out tablets of watered-down steroids. The machines stamped the tablets with a "C" to give the erroneous impression that the drugs had come from a very large, legitimate pharmaceutical company. The tablets were then packaged and given batch numbers and bar codes. They looked just like legitimate steroids. During the raid, the police went through three warehouses and found that many of the fake steroids had been shipped to the United States.

Within the United States

Teen and older users seldom have trouble finding anabolic steroids. Most illicit anabolic steroids are sold at gyms, at competitions, and through mail operations. For the most part, these substances are smuggled into the United States from other countries. The illegal market includes various preparations intended for human and veterinary use as well as counterfeit products. The most common anabolic steroids on the illegal market include testosterone, nandrolone, methenolone, stanozolol, and methandrostenolone. Other steroids seen in the illegal market include boldenone, fluxoymesterone, methandriol, methyltestosterone, oxandrolone, oxymetholone, and trenbolone.

Some adults who work out in gyms or health clubs or go to various athletic competitions sell steroids to teens. Sometimes a gym owner sells them. Some doctors and veterinarians unethically write steroid prescriptions for unethical coaches who want their teen athletes to bulk up quickly. Mail-order sources outside the United States, whether through magazines, newspapers, or the Internet, sell dozens of different steroids illegally. These mail-order businesses can send steroids to cities or towns across the United States without a prescription.

Teens sometimes sell steroids to other teens. According to a 1992 *U.S. News and World Report* article, one quarter of teens who use steroids say they also sell the drugs. One senior high school student in Virginia said that he and a friend stole steroids from a drugstore. Both worked there. They then sold the stolen drugs at school and made a lot of money.[2]

Some teens find that the challenge of getting illegal steroids is exciting. A teen from Iowa, age seventeen, said that he met dealers in parking lots. Before he bought, he would taste test the drugs to see if they were real.[3] Buyers have to be experienced to do this, otherwise they can be fooled by the fake steroids. Most teens do not realize that many of the illegal steroids they buy are fake because they do not contain any active ingredients.[4]

Because most black market steroids are made outside the United States, buyers do not know if they are buying the real drugs. Counterfeiters sometimes duplicate the containers of legitimate steroids. But they do not duplicate the contents. Fake steroids contain no or only tiny amounts of steroids. The fake steroids may be mixed with other drugs or substances. For example, one teen in Chicago spent thousands of dollars for liquid steroids. Instead, he bought a mixture of salt and water. Sometimes penicillin or veterinary drugs are falsely sold as steroids.

Counterfeiters usually mix vegetable oil with alcohol to duplicate liquid steroids. They add the alcohol to destroy bacteria. That is a safety measure, since counterfeiters seldom sterilize or clean their facilities or containers. So, steroid abusers can develop infections from unclean drugs or containers.

Some counterfeiters are fairly sophisticated. The average buyer seldom can tell if the steroids they bought are real or fake. One FBI raid netted a high-volume steroid distribution operation in Michigan. This dealer bought the bottles, caps, and stoppers for his fake steroids from a company that also supplied many legitimate pharmaceutical companies. So, his steroid containers looked real. He also had the labels, boxes, and package inserts professionally printed. Again, they looked real.

The dealer had some problems with imprinting the lot number and expiration date on the box and bottle label. At first, he used a hand stamp. Then he developed a computer program to print this information out on his printer. In just two years, this dealer made over 73,500 vials and bottles of fake steroids to sell on the black market.

Challenge to Law Enforcement

One reason illegal smuggling seems to be worth the risk is that the United States does not mete out much punishment for illegal sales. The federal sentencing guidelines—the punishment enforced if caught selling or distributing illegal steroids—is based on the amount of steroid someone possesses. For example, a single dose of steroids is defined as fifty pills or tablets. Jail time, then, is light, even if someone is caught with hundreds or thousands of pills.

Another reason the steroid black market is booming is the Drug Enforcement Agency and its caseload. Enforcement agents are having a difficult time handling the problems of imports, distribution, sales, and use of all illegal drugs, including cocaine and heroin.

Anabolic steroids are one more drug that the government must deal with. In January 1991, under the Steroid Trafficking Act passed by the United States Congress, steroids were brought under the jurisdiction of the DEA. The DEA has worked hard to try to control the black market steroid trade.

Bringing steroids into the United States is illegal. Customs inspectors can inspect people who want to cross from Mexico into the United States. They typically focus on terrorists and weapons of mass destruction. They also look for cocaine, amphetamines, and marijuana. They are finding more illegal steroids. In 2000, customs agents made nearly nine thousand arrests involving steroids with a street value of $38 million. That is an increase of nearly 50 percent from 1999.[5]

It has proven to be a tough battle. Steroids make a profitable and fairly easy form of drug dealing. Drug dealers have told researchers how easy it is to obtain the drugs and then sell them. There are not enough federal authorities to stop the flow of steroids into gyms and high schools across the United States.

The BALCO Scandal

In February 2004, the federal government brought charges against a personal trainer, a track coach, and two executives of Bay Area Laboratory Co-operative (BALCO), a drug manufacturer. The four men were indicted for distributing illegal drugs, including anabolic steroids, between December 2001 and September 2003. The prosecutors claimed they had provided steroids to many athletes, including track and field competitors and professional baseball, football, and hockey players.[6]

According to a report in the *San Francisco Chronicle*, baseball star Barry Bonds had received steroids from BALCO through his personal trainer. Jason Giambi and Gary Sheffield of the New York Yankees were also named in the article as players who were involved. All three men denied using steroids.[7] As of March 2004, the investigation was continuing.

8

Continuing Controversy, New Solutions

Steroids and steroidlike substances are used by athletes and others who want to perfect their bodies. Since steroids went on the federal controlled-substance list, their legal manufacture in the United States has been restricted greatly. Yet steroids are easily available to those who want them and are willing to pay for them. Why is this? The illegal anabolic steroid demand is huge and the profits are great for drug traders. The steroid supplement market also has exploded since 1998.

Booming Black Market for Steroids

The heavy demand for steroids has created a black market. Illegal steroid sales top

99

more than $500 million each year.[1] For example, at one time, a kilogram (2.2 pounds) of testosterone could be bought legally for $500. On the black market, that same amount sold for $24,000. That is big profit. Someone in an illegal laboratory could then take that kilogram of testosterone, mix it with calcium and press the mixture into tablets. The illegal tablets could be sold for about $100,000, an even greater profit.

A spokesperson for the DEA said, "We see factories all over the world producing amounts clearly in excess of any legitimate need, but they're only meeting market demand. This is a consumer-driven operation."[2]

Make Steroids Legal?

One way to counter the booming black market is to make steroids legal, both in society and in sports. Proponents of this idea claim that since some athletes already use steroids, this would make it fair to all. Because of the laws today, unequal access to these drugs means an unfair advantage exists. Also, making steroids legal would end the law-enforcement costs and efforts associated with steroid use. One doctor, for example, who supports legalizing steroids, said the way to handle this is for doctors to monitor athletes who use them. This would put doctors in the position of trying to reduce the harm of steroids.

For steroids to become legal, two major changes would need to take place. Federal and state laws regarding the import, distribution, and prescription of steroids would need to be changed. Also, the ban on steroids in nearly all sports would have to be dropped.

Arguments against making steroids legal are the following:

- Athletes may feel forced to take steroids, drugs known to be harmful, to compete with steroid users.

- These drugs can help develop muscles in the short run, but they can damage health in the long run. No one knows exactly what a user could develop due to steroid abuse, but why take chances with something known to cause major health problems?

- The ideals of sportsmanship and competition would be tossed aside. These drugs can give users an unfair advantage over nonusers. Using steroids is cheating.

Richard L. Sandlin, former assistant coach at the University of Alabama, believed that he could not win without steroids.

> I took steroids from 1976 to 1983. In the middle of 1979, my body began turning a yellowish color. I was very aggressive and combative, had high blood pressure and testicular atrophy (shrinking). I was hospitalized twice with near kidney failure, liver tumors, and severe personality disorders. During my second hospital stay, the doctor found I had become sterile. Two years after I quit using and started training without drugs, I set six new world records in power lifting, something I thought was impossible without the steroids.[3]

These amateur soccer players are simply enjoying the sport. Unfortunately, some athletes seek a competitive edge by using steroids.

Athlete Cindy Olavarri took steroids, even though she admitted that she knew she was cheating. In 1984, the International Olympic Committee announced that the 1984 Games would feature women's cycling. This was the first time this event would appear in the Olympics. Olavarri, a competitive racer since 1979, set her goal—she had to make the Olympic team.

"I decided I would do whatever it took," she said. So, in addition to working out, she began using steroids to gain an unfair advantage. She took these illegal drugs for three and a half years. She suffered liver inflammation, joint and ligament damage, acne, and lots of hair growth on her face. She also stopped menstruating and developed a cancerous back tumor.

None of these health problems stopped Olavarri from using steroids. Olavarri made the team in the Olympic trials. She celebrated her success, then began to prepare for the Games in Colorado. But one phone call changed everything. She was told she had tested positive for steroids and could no longer compete in the Olympics.

"I knew I was cheating," she admitted, but she had set her heart on winning and was willing to take illegal drugs. Olavarri said, "I forgot my values. I'd been tested before and never gotten caught." If she had not been caught in 1984, Olavarri said, "I probably would've taken steroids until I was too sick to continue."

Olavarri takes full responsibility for her actions. She used steroids as a substitute for her self-confidence. She regrets what she did. "My whole athletic career is tarnished, because I'll never know what was the drug and what was me. That's the hardest part—wondering if I could have made the Olympic team without steroids."[4] She will wonder her entire life.

As will Ben Johnson, the Canadian sprinter. No one will ever know whether Johnson won because of steroid use. Perhaps these drugs helped him run faster than the others, and he would not have won without them. Coach Charlie Francis told Johnson that "he would not be able to compete at the world level without using steroids."[5] Charlie Francis was Johnson's coach during the 1988 Summer Olympic Games.

The bottom line is that steroid users are cheaters and lawbreakers. They take illegal shortcuts. According to Arnold Schwarzenegger, head of both former President Bush and former President Clinton's Council on Physical Fitness and Sports, "There is no shortcut."[6]

Schwarzenegger, born in Graz, Austria, on July 30, 1947, started bodybuilding at age fifteen. He used steroids during the 1970s, when he won the Mr. Olympia title six times in a row from 1970 to 1975. He went on to make several movies in the late 1970s, then again in the 1980s and 1990s. Schwarzenegger eventually went public about his steroid use. According to his publicist Pat Kingsley, "Arnold hasn't done steroids since they were made illegal," in 1990.[7]

Should the United States Regulate Steroidlike Supplements?

In 1998, St. Louis Cardinals baseball player Mark McGwire successfully broke Roger Maris's home-run record by hitting 70 home runs. After he told news reporters that he used the steroidal supplement androstenedione, an andro craze developed in the United States. Though andro and similar substances are banned by some sports organizations, they are permitted in baseball and other sports. Explained a conditioning trainer at a gym, "If it's legal and you're in a sport that demands size, speed, and strength, you have to take it. Your income depends on it."[8]

But questions about andro remain. First is the issue of whether andro is a steroid. The substance appears to boost testosterone levels and seems to produce the same or similar side effects as anabolic steroids. Manufacturers of andro and other steroid-like supplements claim that their substances can build muscles and improve strength and stamina, or endurance. Most countries have already decided that andro is a steroid and have banned it. If deemed a steroid in the United States, then andro would fall under the Anabolic Steroids Control Act of 1990, which restricts these drugs.

Currently, andro and other steroid supplements are referred to as dietary supplements. They are not regulated by the United States Food and Drug Administration or any other regulatory agency. That is because these drugs do not treat, cure, or diagnose a disease.

Second is an ethical issue. Many say that McGwire's achievements will be lessened because he used a drug.

There is a third issue. According to Dr. Linn Goldberg, professor of medicine at Oregon Health

Elected governor of California in 2003, former steroid user Arnold Schwarzenegger now speaks against drug use and in support of a healthy lifestyle.

Sciences University, "Studies show that supplements are gateway substances to steroid use. Kids who use them are at greater risk for using anabolic steroids."[9]

Change Society's Values: Winning at All Costs Is Not OK

One of the basic steroid abuse issues that needs examining is the existing American social environment. Many in our society teach that sports are not just about fun. Instead, winning is the all-important end result of playing any competition. Many players believe that "winning isn't everything, it's the only thing."[10] This is the way competition works and is often viewed in our society, which leads some to unhealthy behaviors such as steroid use.

Americans have long thrived on competition, both in business and in sports. However, often in American society, competition usually means beating other people, and if possible, coming in first. That does not mean winning all the time, an impossible goal anyway. In a race, only one person wins, unless two or more hit the finish line at the exact same time. So in most competitions there is a winner and others who come in second, third, fourth, fifth, and so on.

Yet many in our society seem to consider winning the only goal of competition. This sets up an "us" against "them" or "me" against "him/her" competition. It is all about beating someone else. If this is true, people can justify, or can be lead to believe, that one should win at any cost. To win, one can justify anything, including the use of steroids.

To win at any cost is not a new concept. Records from the ancient Greek Olympics show that winners were well rewarded with money. As a result, some athletes cheated to get these monetary rewards. College athletics have long documented histories of cheaters. Today's news media has widely broadcast to today's teens that anabolic steroids and other performance-enhancing drugs have helped many modern athletes achieve their goals.

Competition is better defined as being the best you can in something you undertake. A healthy view of competition is to try your hardest and produce the best work you can. With this viewpoint, people try to best their own best time, improve their batting average, learn new skills, or challenge themselves to improve. Another type of competition is to compete against an objective standard such as par in golf or a "10" in gymnastics. Beyond competition is the importance of having fun, working with others toward a common goal, and getting exercise.

Change Society's Values:
It Is OK to Look Like Yourself

There is another societal concern today that feeds into steroid abuse—the fixation on the muscularity of men. Many males and females aspire to look like their favorite muscular movie star or athlete. Well-known wrestlers, bodybuilders, and athletes such as "Stone Cold" Steve Austin and Mark McGwire create dreams of bulging muscles in teens. Bodybuilder, movie star, and former steroid user Arnold Schwarzenegger, continues to show off his muscles on the movie screen.

To many, this fixation on bulging muscles sends an inappropriate message to teens. The message is that money, reward, and fame are to be gained at any price, including the use of illegal drugs.

How does our society deal with these inappropriate messages? National experts say that change is necessary and that this change must come from all of us. Harrison G. Pope, Katharine A. Phillips, and Roberto Olivardia are authors of the book *The Adonis Complex: The Secret Crisis of Male Body Obsession*. Their book is the first to address a health crisis among people of all ages—the male obsession with appearance, which is fed by steroids. They wrote *The*

Adonis Complex based on original research involving more than a thousand men over fifteen years.

In their book, these three national experts provide five basic points to counter the current trend of inappropriate body messages:

- Do not fall for media images. These images are all around us—on television, on the Internet, in the movies. The average person sees many of these media messages each day, claiming that the ideal male body is lean and muscular. That is only an ideal, not real life. The vast majority of people can never attain this ideal.

- Many super-muscular males are actually products of drugs such as anabolic steroids. This is a steroid hoax. Drug use helps create these muscular bodies.

- A huge industry profits from making people feel insecure about their bodies. Each year, manufacturers and sellers make billions of dollars from hawking products that supposedly improve the body's appearance. This includes steroids and also hair replacements, penis enlargements, protein supplements, and so on. Some ads feature a male model who probably has used steroids. However, using a particular product probably will not make a teen look like a model.

- Being masculine or feminine is not about how anyone looks. Self-worth and confidence are not built on appearance alone. These are values learned and held by each person.

- It is OK to look like yourself. Artificial means like steroids produce an artificial person. Once a person stops taking steroids, the outward appearance changes. Instead of being taken in by phony messages that males and females must look lean, muscular, and buff, instead, teens need to be comfortable with how their bodies really are.[11]

Play Safe, Play Fair

Success in sports, school, and in your long-term goals takes talent, skill, practice, and hard work. "If you ask elite athletes in any sport what they did to get to the top, they often break it down to the basics—training, conditioning, and practice," said Dr. Edward R. Laskowski, codirector of the Sports Medicine Center at the Mayo Clinic in Rochester, Minnesota.

He continued,

I think there's a danger that kids will think: "If I want to be like him [an elite athlete], I'll need to take something." I think we always tend to look for an external agent as a magic bullet, a magic pill that's going to help us perform. The truth is, there isn't any.[12]

Using steroids to improve strength, performance, or to pack on big muscles is cheating. In sports, it interferes with fair competition. Anabolic steroids are dangerous to your health, both short-term and long-term.

Major sports figures speak out against steroid use. This includes bodybuilding greats such as Arnold Schwarzenegger and Lee Haney, former

Young athletes can develop their skills through practice and proper training. And though winning games is important, having fun is, too.

professional wrestler Jesse Ventura, and Steve Courson, a former offensive lineman in the National Football League. Major magazines such as *Sports Illustrated, Time,* and *Newsweek* have published articles to warn their readers about the dangers of steroid abuse.

Some young people surf the Internet to find information about how to buy and use steroids. Much of this information is incorrect or incomplete. These Web sites may tell readers what steroids to take, but they often do not discuss the harmful side effects. Some steroids promoted on the Internet may be illegal. Do not believe everything you read or see on the Internet, especially about anabolic steroids.

Drug-Free Training Tips

By taking steroids, you try to impose an unrealistic look onto your body. Your body is genetically programmed to be a certain size, and even taking massive dosages of steroids will not change your body safely and permanently.

There are many healthy ways to improve your appearance or increase your strength. Here are some ideas:

- Avoid alcohol, tobacco use, and illegal drugs. Also stay away from over-the-counter drugs that promise quick fixes to bulking up and performance enhancement.

- Train safely and use proper form. Poor form leads to poor results and injuries that will keep you out of the gym. Find a reliable and knowledgeable professional to help you train. Listen to and follow that person's coaching and training recommendations.

- Avoid overtraining. Some people train two hours a day, doing two dozen or more exercises per body part. That is overtraining. Professional bodybuilders do not train that extensively.

- Eat a healthy diet, one that is balanced and varied. Eat a good balance of protein to build muscles and carbohydrates for energy. Keep away from fried foods and fast foods.

- Drink plenty of water. When you are training, you need to drink a gallon of water daily. Sodas do not count.

- Get plenty of sleep.

- Play safely and use protective gear to avoid injuries.

- Talk to your doctor about nutrition, your health, injury prevention, and safe ways to build strength and endurance.

- Keep a realistic outlook and be patient. Realize that there is no quick and easy way to win or reach your goals. It takes practice and hard work. Professional trainers recommend gaining one pound of muscle per month by following a proper training and exercise regime.

- Set realistic goals. Be proud of your progress. Many people say that it is not winning that is important, but the steps you take to reach your goals.

So, make the most of what you have. Most young people who are patient and dedicated can develop a physique they will be proud of if they follow a sound plan. Use a two-prong commonsense approach to working out: a healthy diet and a consistent workout plan. You will see positive results this way. Plus, you will gain real self-esteem—rather than fake confidence resulting from steroid use.

Chapter Notes

Chapter 1. Making World Headlines

1. Sylvain Blanchard, "Ben Johnson on the Record," *Maclean's*, July 29, 1996, p. 39.

2. Mayo Foundation for Medical Education and Research, "Teens and Steroids: Drug Use Rising Despite Dangers," August 9, 2001, <http://www.mayo clinic.com/findinfo...95A16A44C032F92532> (November 30, 2001).

3. Phil Wallace, "Use of Ephedra Supplements, Steroids Up, NCAA Says," *Food Chemical News*, August 20, 2001, p. 12.

Chapter 2. What Are Anabolic Steroids?

1. Wasim Rashid, "Testosterone Abuse and Affective Disorders," *Journal of Substance Abuse Treatment*, vol. 18, 2000, p. 179.

2. "Anabolic Behavior," *Chemist and Druggist*, September 18, 1999, <http://web2.infotrac.galegroup. com...n_21_O_A56081357?sw_aep=mnauduluth> (December 12, 2001).

3. Title 21, United States Code, Section 802 (41); 21 Code of Federal Regulations, Section 1306.04(a).

4. "Anabolic Behavior."

5. Gayle Newshan and Wade Leon, "The Use of Anabolic Agents in HIV Disease," *International Journal of STD and AIDS*, 2001, p. 144.

6. Trent Tschirgi, "Do Anabolic Steroids Have Any Legitimate Medical Uses?" University of Maryland Office of Substance Abuse Studies, 1992, <http://

www.cesar.umd.edu/www2root/metnet/docs/roida4a.
txt> (December 20, 2001).

7. Mayo Clinic, "Muscle-Building Supplements. Are They Safe?" November 30, 2001, <http://www.mayo clinic.com/invoke.cfm?id=HQ01105> (May 30, 2001).

8. Ibid.

9. Jennifer Longley and Charles Yesalis, "Hazard Alert," *People Weekly*, October 12, 1998, p. 143.

Chapter 3. Who Is Using?

1. Steven Ungerleider, "Steroids: Youth at Risk," *Harvard Mental Health Letter*, May 2001, p. 4.

2. B. W. Corder, et al., "Trends in drug use behavior at ten Central Arizona high schools," *Arizona Journal of Health, Physical Education, Recreation, and Dance*, 1975, pp. 10–11.

3. W. Buckley, et al., "Estimated Prevalence of Anabolic Steroid Use Among Male High School Student Seniors," *Journal of the American Medical Association*, vol. 260, no. 23, 1988, pp. 3441–3445.

4. Ibid.

5. R. H. DuRant, et al., "Use of Multiple Drugs Among Adolescents Who Use Anabolic Steroids," *New England Journal of Medicine*, vol. 328, no. 13, April 1, 1993, p. 922.

6. Patrick Zickler, "Annual Survey Finds Increasing Teen Use of Ecstasy, Steroids," *NIDA NOTES*, May 2000, <http://165.112.78.61/NIDA_Notes/NNVol16N2/ Annual.html> (December 7, 2001).

7. U.S. Department of Justice, Drug Enforcement Agency, "Steroids: Fast Facts," July 2003, <http://www. usdoj.gov/ndic/pub5/5448/index.htm> (December 23, 2003).

8. Mike Fish, "Women in Sports: Growing Pains— Gains from Steroids Enticing Female Athletes," *The Atlanta Constitution*, September 23, 1998, p. D09.

9. "Anabolic Steroid Use Rising Among Teenage Girls; Stable Among Boys," press release, Penn State

University, December 15, 1977, <http://www.psu.edu/ur/NEWS/girlsteroid.html> (December 4, 2001).

10 "Anabolic Steroid Use," *NIDA Research Report*, November 11, 2001, <http://165.112.78.61/ResearchReports/Steroids/anabolicsteroids2.html> (December 2, 2001).

11. Ibid.

12. Robert Mathias, "Steroid Prevention Program Scores with High School Athletes," *NIDA Notes*, July/August 1997, p. 15.

13. "Anabolic Steroid Use."

14. Holcomb B. Noble, "Steroid Use by Teen-Age Girls Is Rising," *New York Times*, June 1, 1999, p. F8.

15. Joannie M. Schrof, "Pumped Up," *U.S. News and World Report*, June 1, 1992, p. 61.

16. Stacey Pamela Patton, "Steroid Shock," *Scholastic Choices*, p. 8, November–December 2001, <http://web5.infotrac.galegroup.com...rn_1_0_A80366213?sw_aep=umn_duluth> (December 12, 2001).

17. James Deacon, "Biceps in a Bottle," *Maclean's*, May 2, 1994, p. 52.

18. Office of National Drug Control Policy, "Drug Facts: Steroids," 2001, <http://www.whitehouse drugpolicy.gov/drugfact/steroids/index.html> (December 28, 2001).

19. Charles E. Yesalis, ed., *Anabolic Steroids in Sport and Exercise* (Champaign, Ill.: Human Kinetics, 2000), p. 19.

20. Ibid., p. 94.

21. Don H. Catlin and Thomas H. Murray, "Performance-Enhancing Drugs, Fair Competition, and Olympic Sport," *Journal of the American Medical Association*, vol. 276, no. 3, July 1996, pp. 231–237.

22. T. Dezelsky, J. Toohey, R. Shaw, "Nonmedical Drug Use Behavior at Five United States Universities: A 15-Year Study," *Bulletin on Narcotics*, vol. 27, 1985, pp. 45–53.

••

23. Yesalis, pp. 90–91.

24. W. A. Anderson, et al., "A National Survey of Alcohol and Drug Use by College Athletes," *The Physician and Sportsmedicine*, vol. 19, 1991, pp. 91–104.

25. Phil Wallace, "Use of Ephedra Supplements, Steroids Up, NCAA Says," *Food Chemical News*, vol. 43, August 20, 2001, p. 12.

Chapter 4. Health Consequences

1. Cynthia Kuhn, Scott Swartzwelder, and Wilkie Wilson, *Pumped: Straight Facts for Athletes about Drugs, Supplements, and Training* (New York: W.W. Norton & Company, 2000), p. 76; and "Are Steroids Worth the Risk?" December 1999, <http://www.kidshealth.org/PageMana...1&ps=207&cat_id=&article_set= 22136> (December 4, 2001).

2. Rick Telander and Merrell Noden, "The Death of an Athlete," *Sports Illustrated*, February 20, 1989, pp. 68–72.

3. *Encyclopedia of Drugs, Alcohol, and Addictive Behavior* (New York: Macmillan Reference), 2001, p. 126.

4. "Steroid Abuse," WRAL OnLine, December 2, 2002, <http://www.wral.tv.com/features/health team/1996/0722-steroids> (July 22, 1996).

5. H.M. Sklarek, R.P. Mantovani, and E. Erens, "AIDS in a Bodybuilder Using Anabolic Steroids," *New England Journal of Medicine*, vol. 311, no. 26, 1984, p. 1701.

6. Joannie M. Schrof, "Pumped Up," *U.S. News and World Report*, June 1, 1992, p. 61.

7. Darryl S. Inaba, William E. Cohen, and Michael E. Holstein, *Uppers, Downers, All Arounders: Physical and Mental Effects of Psychoactive Drugs* (Ashland, Oreg.: CNS Publications, Inc., 1997), p. 271.

8. "Steroid Abusers May Go on to Abuse Opioids, Too," *NIDA Notes*, vol. 5, no. 6, 2001, p. 1.

9. Nina Riccio, "Steer Away from Steroids," *Current Health 2*, October 2000, pp. 22–25.

10. Steven Stocker, "Study Provides Additional Evidence That High Steroid Doses Elicit Psychiatric Symptoms in Some Men," *NIDA Notes*, September 2000, <http://165.112.78.61/NIDA_Notes/NNVol154N4/Study.html> (December 7, 2001).

11. Ibid.

12. Ibid.

13. William Nack, "The Muscle Murders," *Sports Illustrated*, May 18, 1998, <http://vweb.hwwilson web.com/cgi-bi...GT.&Sp.URL.P=I(FZZ7)J(0000 442923)> (December 4, 2001).

14. Jere Longman, "Drugs in Sports: An Athlete's Dangerous Experiment," *The New York Times*, November 26, 2003, p. D1.

15. *Encyclopedia of Drugs, Alcohol, and Addictive Behavior*, p. 127.

16. Sean Pitts, "I was lucky to get a wake-up call before it was too late," *Parade Magazine*, November 30, 2003, p. 22.

Chapter 5. Steroids and Body Image

1. James Deacon, "Biceps in a Bottle: Teenagers Turn to Steroids to Build Muscles," *Maclean's*, May 2, 1994, p. 52.

2. Gen Kanayama, Harrison G. Pope, Jr., James I. Hudson, "Body Image Drugs: A Growing Psychosomatic Problem," *Psychotherapy and Psychosomatics*, March/April 2001, p. 62.

3. Sam Wright, Sarah Grogan, Geoff Hunter, "Motivations for Anabolic Steroid Use Among Bodybuilders," *Journal of Health Psychology*, vol. 5, 2000, pp. 566–571.

4. John Cloud, "Never Too Buff," *Time Atlantic*, April 24, 2000, pp. 58–61.

5. Harrison G. Pope, Jr., Katharine A. Phillips, and Roberto Olivardia, *The Adonis Complex: The Secret*

Crisis of Male Body Obsession (New York: The Free Press, 2000), p. 44.

6. Stephen S. Hall, "Obsession for Men," *The New York Times Upfront*, February 14, 2000, p. 15.

7. "Teens and Steroids: Drug Use Rising Despite Dangers," August 9, 2001, <http://www.mayo clinic.com/findinfo...95-A16A44C032F92532> (November 30, 2001).

8. James E. Wright and Virginia S. Cowart, *Anabolic Steroids: Altered States* (Carmel, Ind.: Benchmark Press, 1990), pp. 73–74.

9. Hall, p. 15.

10. Mike Chessler, "The Adonis Complex: A Body Image Disorder of Our Own," 2001, <drDrew.com. article.asp?id=599> (July 28, 2002).

11. James Brady, "In Step With The Rock," *Parade*, March 28, 2004, p. 22.

12. Lesa Rae Vartanian, Carrie L. Giant, Rhonda M. Passino, "Ally McBeal vs. Arnold Schwarzenegger: Comparing Mass Media, Interpersonal Feedback and Gender Predictors of Satisfaction with Body Thinness and Muscularity," *Social Behavior and Personality*, vol. 29, no. 7, 2001, p. 711.

13. Ibid.

14. Ibid.

15. Hall, p. 15.

16. H. G. Pope, Jr., D. L. Katz, and J. I. Hudson, "Anorexia Nervosa and Reverse Anorexia Among 108 Male Bodybuilders," *Comprehensive Psychiatry*, vol. 34, 1993, pp. 406–409.

17. Cloud.

Chapter 6. Steroids and Sports

1. Simon Craig, "Riding High," *History Today*, July 2000, p. 18.

2. Ibid.

3. James E. Wright and Virginia S. Cowart,

Anabolic Steroids: Altered States (Carmel, Ind.: Benchmark Press, 1990), p. 3.

4. "Teens and Steroids: Drug Use Rising Despite Dangers," August 9, 2001, <http://www.mayo clinic.com/findinfo...95-A16A44C032F92532> (November 30, 2001).

5. "Doping Undetected," CBS News, September 17, 2000, <http://cbsnews.cbs.com/now/story/0.1597. 231760-412.00.html> (December 28, 2001).

6. Gregory Stejskal, "They Shoot Horses, Don't They?" *The FBI Law Enforcement Bulletin*, vol. 5, pp. 8–13, August 1994, <http://wwwweb3.infotrac. g...purl=rcl_EAOM_0_A15721487duluth.html> (December 31, 2001).

7. Tom Verducci, et al., "Totally Juiced," *Sports Illustrated*, June 3, 2002, p. 35.

8. Ibid., p. 44.

9. "Teens and Steroids: Drug Use Rising Despite Dangers."

10. Ibid.

11. Edward J. Bird and Gert G. Wagner, "Sport As a Common Property Resource: A Solution to the Dilemmas of Doping," *The Journal of Conflict Resolution*, vol. 41, December 1997, p. 751.

12. Verducci, et al., p. 38.

13. Michael Bamberger and Don Yaeger, "Over the Edge," *Sports Illustrated*, April 14, 1997, p. 61.

14. Ibid.

15. "CNN Year in Review: Sports, April 28, 1995," *CNN.com*, 1995, <http://www.cnn.com/EVENTS/ year_in_review/sports/apr.html> (December 23, 2003.)

16. Werner Franke and Brigitte Berendonk, "Hormonal Doping and Androgenization of Athletes," *Clinical Chemistry*, vol. 33, 1997, p. 1262.

17. Steven Ungerleider, *Faust's Gold: Inside the East German Doping Machine* (New York: St. Martin's Press, 2001), preface.

••

18. Ibid., pp. 10–13.

19. Steven Ungerleider, "Steroids: Youth at Risk," *Harvard Mental Health Letter*, May 2001, p. 4.

20. Ungerleider, p. 177.

21. Bamberger and Yaeger, p. 63.

22. Charles E. Yesalis, "Doping Among Adolescent Athletes," *Balliere's Clinical Endocrinology and Metabolism*, vol. 14, No. 1, 2000, p. 30.

Chapter 7. Laws

1. Skin Rozin, et al., "Steroids: A Spreading Peril," *Business Week*, June 19, 1995, p. 138.

2. Joannie M. Schrof, "Pumped Up," *U.S. News and World Report*, June 1, 1992, p. 61.

3. Ibid.

4. James E. Wright and Virginia S. Cowart, *Anabolic Steroids: Altered States* (Carmel, Ind.: Benchmark Press, 1990), p. 120.

5. Tom Verducci, "Buyer's Market," *Sports Illustrated*, June 3, 2002, p. 46.

6. "Feds Charge 4 in Sports Steroids Scheme: No Indictments Sought Against Athletes," The Associated Press, February 12, 2004.

7. Rob Gloster, The Associated Press, "Bonds, Giambi, Sheffield have no comment on steroid report," *USA Today*, March 3, 2004, <http://usatoday.com/sports/baseball/2004-03-02-bonds-giambi-steorids_x.htm> (April 1, 2004).

Chapter 8. Continuing Controversy, New Solutions

1. Darryl S. Inaba, William E. Cohen, and Michael E. Holstein, *Uppers, Downers, All Arounders: Physical and Mental Effects of Psychoactive Drugs* (Ashland, Oreg.: CNS Publications, Inc, 1997), p. 273.

2. Skin Rozin, et al., "Steroids: A Spreading Peril," *Business Week*, June 19, 1995, p. 138.

3. Inaba, Cohen, and Holstein, p. 271.

4. Marcia J. Pear, "Steroid Roulette," *Women's Sports & Fitness*, October 1992, pp. 18–19.

5. James E. Wright and Virginia S. Cowart, *Anabolic Steroids: Altered States* (Carmel, Ind.: Benchmark Press, 1990), p. 153.

6. Kenneth T. Walsh, "Schwarzenegger Speaks: Steroids Don't Pay Off," *U.S. News & World Report*, June 1, 1992, p. 63.

7. Steve Sailer, "Commentary: A Unique Aspect of Arnold," *Washington Times*, August 15, 2003, <http://washingtontimes.com/upi-breaking/2000811-101222-84174r.htm> (August 29, 2003).

8. "Popping the Muscle Pill," *Maclean's*, September 7, 1998, p. 50.

9. Stephen S. Hall, "Obsession for Men," *The New York Times Upfront*, February 14, 2000, p. 15.

10. Edward J. Bird and Gert G. Wagner, "Sport As a Common Property Resource: A Solution to the Dilemmas of Doping," *The Journal of Conflict Resolution*, vol. 41, December 1997, p. 751.

11. Harrison G. Pope, Katherine A. Phillips, and Roberto Olivarda, *The Adonis Complex: The Secret Crisis of Male Body Obsession* (New York: Free Press, 2000), pp. 239–243.

12. "Muscle-Building Supplements: Are They Safe?" Mayo Clinic Web site, May 30, 2001, <http://www.mayoclinic.com/invoke.cfm?id=HQ01105&printpage=true)> (November 30, 2001).

Glossary

adrenal glands—A pair of organs near the kidneys that produce androgenic hormones.

anabolic—Mimicking the muscle-building effects of the male sex hormone testosterone.

anabolic steroids—Synthetic steroids that increase muscle size and strength. (Also called anabolic-androgenic steroids.)

androgen—A male sex hormone responsible for the development of masculine characteristics such as the growth of body hair and deepening of the voice. Testosterone is one type of androgen.

androgenic—Having or producing masculine features.

black market—An illegal market, or the illegal selling and buying of products or services.

buffed—Having large muscles.

bulking up—Increasing muscle mass through steroids.

carbohydrates—A class of food that includes sugars and starches. Carbohydrates are the main source of energy for animals.

corticosteroids—Synthetic steroids used to treat some health problems; different from anabolic steroids.

cycle—The eight-to-twelve-week period when steroids are used. After that, the user lets his or her body rest for the same period.

doping—A slang term for using steroids to improve athletic performance.

estrogen—A female sex hormone that stimulates the

development of sex characteristics such as breasts and menstruation.

hormones—Naturally produced chemical substances that regulate functions in the body such as growth, sexual development, and reproduction.

juiced—A slang term that describes someone who is using steroids.

megadosing—Taking large amounts of steroids.

plateau—When a steroid no longer works at a certain level.

roider—A slang term for a steroid user who takes the drug only for appearance. Other terms for roider are *juicer* and *joy rider*.

roid rage—A slang term for uncontrolled anger, frustration, or combativeness that results from using anabolic steroids.

shotgunning—A slang term for taking steroids irregularly.

stacking—A slang term for taking several different steroids at the same time.

sterile—Unable to reproduce.

steroids—Chemical substances that regulate functions in the body such as growth. Hormones are one type of steroid.

synthetic—Made from chemicals in a laboratory.

tapering—Slowly decreasing the use of steroids.

tendons—Tissues that attach muscles to bones.

testes—The male reproductive glands that produce sperm and testosterone.

testicular atrophy—Shrinking of the testes.

testosterone—A hormone that causes a boy's body to develop.

withdrawal—The process of ridding the body of a drug.

Further Reading

Books

Connolly, Sean. *Steroids*. Barrington, Ill.: Heinemann Library, 2000.

Dudley, William, editor. *Drugs and Sports*. San Diego: Greenhaven Press, Inc., 2001.

Persico, Deborah A. *Vernonia School District vs. Acton: Drug Testing in Schools*. Berkeley Heights, N.J.: Enslow Publishers, 1999.

Spring, Albert. *Steroids and Your Muscles: The Incredibly Disgusting Story*. New York: The Rosen Publishing Group, Inc., 2001.

Stewart, Gail B. *Drugs and Sports*. Farmington Hills, Mich.: Gale Group, 1998.

Internet Addresses

American Council for Drug Education
<http://www.acde.org>

National Clearinghouse for Alcohol and Drug Information
<http://www.health.org>

National Institute on Drug Abuse
<http://www.nida.nih.gov>
<http://www.steroidabuse.org>

Index